Creativity in Early Childhood Classrooms

The Authors

Deborah W. Tegano is Associate Professor, Department of Child and Family Studies, University of Tennessee, Knoxville.

James D. Moran III is Associate Dean, College of Human Ecology, University of Tennessee, Knoxville; and Child Care Consultant, Child Care Plus, Knoxville.

Janet K. Sawyers is Professor of Child Development and Director, Child Development Laboratories, Department of Family and Child Development, Virginia Polytechnic Institute, Blacksburg.

The Advisory Panel

Bonnie Blanton, Early Childhood Educator, Park View Elementary School, Mooresville, North Carolina

Joseph P. Caliguri, Chair and Professor of Educational Administration, School of Education, University of Missouri at Kansas City

Janice Cerabona, Pre-Kindergarten Teacher, Eliot Elementary School, Maine

Marvin Greenberg, Professor of Music Education, University of Hawaii, Honolulu

J. Cynthia McDermott, Assistant Professor, California State University, Dominguez Hills

Margaret Weiser, Professor, Early Childhood Education, University of Iowa, Iowa City

**NEA
EARLY CHILDHOOD
EDUCATION SERIES**

Creativity in Early Childhood Classrooms

Deborah W. Tegano
James D. Moran III
Janet K. Sawyers

A NATIONAL EDUCATION ASSOCIATION PUBLICATION

Printing History
    First Printing: September 1991

Note

The opinions expressed in this publication should not be construed as representing the policy or position of the National Education Association. Materials published by the NEA Professional Library are intended to be discussion documents for educators who are concerned with specialized interests of the profession.

Library of Congress Cataloging-in-Publication Data

Tegano, Deborah W.
    Creativity in early childhood classrooms / Deborah W. Tegano,
James D. Moran III, Janet K. Sawyers.
        p.   cm. —(NEA Early childhood education series)
    ISBN 0-8106--0358-6
    1. Early childhood education—United States.   2. Creative ability
in children—United States.   I. Moran, James D.   II. Sawyers, Janet
K.   III. Title.   IV. Series: Early childhood education series.
LB1139.25.T44   1991
372.21—dc20   91–19440
                                                            CIP

CONTENTS

Chapter 1

INTRODUCTION

To him whose elastic and vigorous thought
keeps pace with the sun, the day is a perpetual
morning.

—Henry David Thoreau

"A fireman painting a picture of himself." The answer evokes imagery, a level of imagination, a real fascination. Four-and-a- half-year-old Taylor Allison was calmly sitting at a small table in a research room responding to our inquiry "Tell me all the things you can think of that are red." This and thousands of other responses from children around the country have convinced us that the precursors of creativity are clearly evident in young children, and that teachers play a crucial role in the nurturing of creative abilities.

WHY STUDY CREATIVITY IN YOUNG CHILDREN?

Creativity involves adaptability and flexibility of thought. These are the same types of skills that numerous reports on education (e.g., the Carnegie Report 1986) have suggested are critical for students. Although creativity is a multifaceted concept (Runco and Albert 1990; Sternberg 1988), for teachers of young children it may focus on problem solving. But creativity is a special type of problem solving—one that involves problems for which there are no easy answers: that is, problems for which popular or conventional responses do not work. Thus, adaptability and flexibility of thought may characterize children who come up with creative or original ideas. "Tell me all the things you can think of that are red" may lead to responses such as "cold hands," "chicken pox," as well as Taylor's "a fireman painting a picture of himself," reflecting fluency, flexibility, and adaptability of thought.

// Just as all children are not equally intelligent, all children are not equally creative. But just as all children exhibit behaviors that evidence intelligence from birth, they also exhibit behaviors that evidence the potential for creativity. We know that by constructing the environment we can encourage (or discourage) the expression of creativity; by constructing our curricula, we can enhance children's creative skills; and by increasing our understanding, we can heighten our sensitivity to creative expression. \\

Early childhood teachers have the opportunity to enhance creativity skills in all children in their classrooms. This is the major thrust of this monograph—describing what teachers can do to enhance creative skills. In this chapter we present a brief overview of creativity to set the stage for discussions on the child, the curriculum, the teacher, and the environment. This brief overview provides a framework for the big picture of how we may recognize and facilitate creativity. Examples of how the child, the curriculum, and the teacher make the environment conducive to creative potential will follow in subsequent chapters. *Our goal throughout is to paint a picture of the many faces of the development of creativity in children and to recognize ways to enhance their potential so they will develop confidence in their abilities to meet the challenges of a rapidly changing world.*

WHAT IS CREATIVITY?

Creativity has been considered in terms of process, product, or person (Barron and Harrington 1981), and has been defined as the interpersonal and intrapersonal process by means of which original, high-quality, and genuinely significant products are developed (Sawyer, Moran, and Tegano 1987, 1990). In dealing with young children, the focus should be on

8

the process (i.e., developing and generating original ideas), which is seen as the basis of creative potential. When trying to understand this process, it is helpful to consider Guilford's (1956) differentiation between convergent and divergent thought. Problems requiring convergent thought have one correct solution. Problems requiring divergent thought call for the generation of many solutions, a few of which may be novel or of high quality. We will address this definition in more detail in the second chapter. This focus on process allows the consideration of creativity across the curriculum instead of its usual limitation to art and music activities.

To properly understand children's creativity, the concept of creativity must be differentiated from intelligence and talent. Ward (1974) expressed concern about whether creativity in young children could be differentiated from other cognitive abilities. More recent studies (e.g., Moran, Milgram, Sawyers, and Fu 1983) have shown that components of creative potential can indeed be distinguished from intelligence. The term "gifted" is often used to imply high intelligence. Wallach (1970) has argued that intelligence and creativity are independent of each other; a highly creative child may or may not be highly intelligent. Our work has shown this to be the case. That is, young children of above-average intelligence, at least as measured by standard IQ tests, perform no better on age-appropriate measures of creative potential than do children of average or below-average intelligence.

Creativity goes beyond possession and use of artistic or musical talent. In this context, talent refers to the possession of a high degree of technical skills in a specialized area. Thus, an artist may have wonderful technical skills but may not succeed in evoking the emotional response that makes the viewer feel that a painting, for example, is unique. It is important to keep in mind that creativity is evidenced not only in music, art, or writing, but through the curriculum, in science, social studies, and other areas.

Our perspective also leads us to investigate how context and environment influence the expression of creative behavior. We postulate that individual characteristics (e.g., *biological* variables such as gender or hemispheric dominance; *cognitive* variables such as fantasy or attention; and *personality* variables such as risk-taking, conformity, and temperament), as well as environmental variables (including *cultural* lifestyles and expectations, and *contextual* variables such as play opportunities, reward, and parent and teacher behaviors), all play a part in the development of creativity (Sawyers, Moran, and Tegano 1990). See Figure 1.

The relationships depicted in this model are dynamic and primarily directed through context. Thus, in any particular situation the personality or cognitive or cultural or biological variables may be expressed in a different fashion depending on the context. In other words, *what happens in the early childhood classroom does make a difference.*

Figure 1
Developmental Ecological Model
of Creative Potential in Young Children

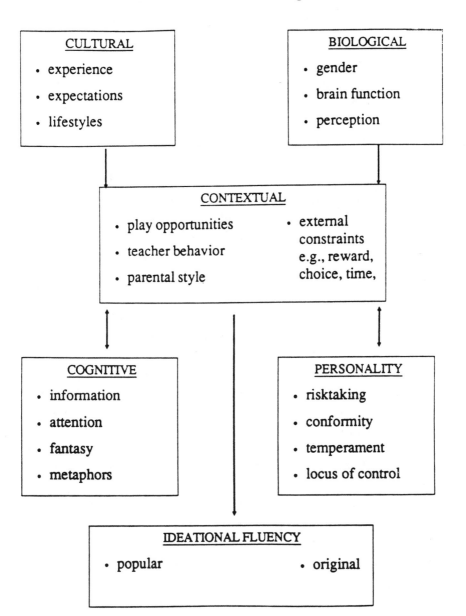

HOW CAN WE FOSTER CREATIVITY?

The atmosphere of the classroom, the attitudes of the teacher, and the aptitudes of the students all play a part in fostering creativity. As we elaborate on the key features in subsequent chapters, our focus is on children ages three to eight. The past 30 years have witnessed a tremendous increase in our knowledge and understanding of the construct of creativity, yet little of the theory or research has focused on how to apply this information to young children. Recent research has been clear in pointing out what teachers may do to *squelch* creativity at a young age (e.g., Hennessey and Amabile 1987); as teachers, we can warn our colleagues to avoid certain pitfalls. (See "How to Kill Creativity" in the Appendix). With this valuable knowledge in perspective, we have tried to extend this monograph and focus on what teachers *can do* to *foster* creativity in early childhood classrooms—that is, to provide a proactive approach to creativity in early childhood education.

Exploration, play, and creative expression are an integral part of the preschool and primary grade curriculum. It is the position of the authors and others in teacher education, however, that this conception of teaching should not stop in third grade. Elementary science educators (Hawkins 1983), for example, have long espoused a need for discovery learning throughout the science curriculum as discovery learning embodies the essence of the scientific method, a way of thinking that is useful throughout life (Cronin 1989). Likewise, other educators grounded in Piagetian theory are convinced that there is a place for experiential learning throughout all elementary grades as well as middle school, high school, and even the preparation of teachers at the university level (Fosnot 1990). Thus, we hope that early childhood educators do not feel isolated as they begin to initiate steps to enhance creativity in their children.

Teaching to facilitate creativity is not a recipe approach; it is an attitude toward, perhaps even a philosophy of, teaching.

12

Discovery or inquiry-based learning (Hawkins 1983, Orlich 1989), experientially based constructivist curricula (DeVries and Kohlberg 1990; Kamii 1990), and developmentally appropriate practices in early childhood education (Bredekamp 1987) provide models for teaching young children in which *play and creativity* are an integral part. Thus, the ideas presented here are not meant to revolutionize the early childhood curriculum. Instead, the message might be: *Take what we know is developmentally appropriate curricula for early childhood, and recognize and optimize the opportunities for facilitating creative potential throughout the day.* That is, interpret curriculum guides to facilitate exploration, play, and creative potential. Such interpretation involves teachers assuming an active role in the creative process.

Unfortunately, many of us teach as we were taught (Fosnot 1990); as a result, we may be less likely to encourage children to construct knowledge, think creatively, or feel confident in their problem-solving abilities because *we* have not generally experienced learning from this perspective. Yet, as adults, when we look back on our favorite classroom experiences—courses where we *learned* the most—we find that these experiences probably were not "lecture and test-type" courses. They often contained elements of divergent thinking, discussion, and debate about the "best way," hands-on experiences, and opportunities for us to *learn* rather than to be *taught* any particular concept. We recall, for example, a high school biology class where the interrelatedness of every system of the body was *discovered* and *learned* through the laborious process of dissecting laboratory specimens and the informal comparisons of findings among the students in class, rather than *memorized* by looking at diagrams or reading a textbook.

This is not to say that the knowledge and skills to be acquired (i.e., the curriculum) were not predetermined by the instructor of our favorite course. The necessary or appropriate knowledge and skills are dictated by the nature of the course, but, at the same time, the process of learning may be governed by the principles discussed in this monograph. These key concepts include:

> Opportunities for learning that are somewhat unstructured and provide time for exploration of the concept;

> Ample time for playing with how the concept may be used or applied;

> Environments where judgment is deferred and all ideas are respected, and where discussions and debates are a means of testing ideas in a nonthreatening atmosphere.

Contrast this classroom to the one in which information is presented, albeit very clearly and concisely, and students are tested on how well they can remember and apply the information to a contrived situation. In which classroom are *students* better prepared to face future unfamiliar situations? Which *teacher* promotes an interest in learning? In which *classroom* is creative thinking fostered?

Chapter 2

THE CHILD: DEVELOPMENTAL CHARACTERISTICS OF CREATIVE POTENTIAL

It is most likely that highly curious, intense, and independent children elicit an involvement, an interested response from those around them. The encouragement that they receive from caring adults is in turn an important part of the development of their sense of self, for an inner belief in one's self is a necessary strength in the pursuit of a creative life.
(John-Steiner 1985, 199)

Perhaps the first step in understanding the developmental characteristics of creative potential is deciding what creativity is. The term means many things to many people, probably because creativity itself is so diverse. How can one define a term that is used to describe both Albert Einstein and Jim Henson? We remain fascinated by the term "creativity," especially when we see evidence of it in the children in our classrooms. Much theory and research have been dedicated to defining creativity, but most explanations do not apply to young children. This leads to two questions: "What is creativity in the early childhood years?" and "What are the characteristics of creative young children?"

CREATIVITY IN THE EARLY CHILDHOOD YEARS

One way of defining creativity is to determine how creative potential will be judged—that is, by what criteria will we call something creative? Is it creativity when a child comes to

15

school attired in unusual combinations of clothes and accessories, or when a child seems to be full of crazy or silly ideas? Is it creativity when a child finds a new way to solve an old problem or creates a picture that is *full* of metaphoric images and evokes strong emotions? Creative potential may be seen in all these examples and may appear in different forms in children of different ages. It becomes important to recognize how creativity changes at different levels of development. Most people have ideas about what creativity is in adulthood, but what might we look for in a seventh grader or a kindergarten child? It is important for early childhood teachers to see this whole picture.

This chapter provides information about the development of creativity for early childhood educators. For young children, the critical criterion for creative potential is *originality*. Thus, those who work with young children must understand the *process that leads to original thinking.*

Originality

Originality can be illustrated in a kindergarten classroom where children were making collages from pieces of torn tissue paper. On this particular day the teacher observed Olisa's experimentation with the material and her discovery of a way to make three-dimensional bumps in the collage. Olisa's discovery of the three-dimensional aspect is a form of originality. Though making three-dimensional collages is certainly not a new idea in a kindergarten classroom, it is an original idea for that particular child at that particular time. Consider another kindergarten classroom where the children were embellishing the full-size outlines of their bodies. Most children were adding hair, faces, and clothes to their outlines, while Brett was observed making an original internal drawing of his skeleton.

Process over Product

Let's return to the child with the three-dimensional

16

collage. Teachers of young children are grounded in the "process-over-product" philosophy. Consequently, the teacher's observation of the *process* that leads to originality (exploration and experimentation with the materials) is more valuable than any *judgment of the product* (the three-dimensional bump may have been imperfect and collapsed in the end). Remember that young children do not always have the skills to make a creative product (an elaborate painting or a workable invention), and so it is the process that leads to originality that is the focus of creative potential.

Most preschool and primary grade classrooms are replete with examples of the process of original thinking. We see complex dramas unfold as children act out plays of their own design, clever routes to solutions for math problems, unique interpersonal problem solving, and metaphoric images that astound us.

Creativity in Older Children and Adolescents

Because ours is a developmental definition of creativity, we have included a brief explanation of how the judgment of creativity may change over time. To identify creativity in adolescence and middle childhood, we turn our attention to the criteria of high-quality original products or solutions. Although we cannot forget that products are important for creativity, we need to remind ourselves that this element emerges later in the child's development. An example of this is seen in the projects at a middle school science fair. It becomes very apparent that given equal quality in the rigor and presentation of the research projects, some of the adolescent contestants' ideas for such projects are more unusual than others. For example, a student who created and tested a new chair design may seem to have an idea of a different quality from that of a student who investigated the question of which commercial cleaning product worked most effectively.

At this developmental level, then, creativity is judged by:

original products, or
original solutions.

More than generation of ideas is involved in the creation of products. With older children and adults, self-evaluation leads to refinement and success in problem solving. Prior to the judgment of significance must come a product that is first original; this standard applies at this level.

Creativity in Adults

For adults, creativity is seen in products or solutions that are both original and genuinely significant for society. Marconi's radio, O'Keefe's canvases, Disney's animation, as well as Madeline L'Engle's *Wrinkle in Time* and Shel Silverstein's poetry, are all twentieth century examples of widely recognized creative achievement. If *genuine significance* is our criterion, we can add such ideas as Darwin's theory of natural selection or Watson and Crick's discovery of the helical model of DNA as original conceptions that have made a genuinely significant impact on society and so are considered creative by adult standards.

Thus, as we define creativity for adults, there must be

originality
product
significance

Abstract

By describing adult creativity, we have given a picture of how the definition becomes more focused at younger ages. By considering the younger ages, we provide a better picture of how creativity evolves. It is in early childhood that the critical orientation to the *process* of problem solving emerges. The

18

emphasis on multiple ideas or solutions, generated in a nonevaluative atmosphere that produces originality—this is the starting point for adult creativity.

A Developmental Definition

Barron (1988), a noted scholar of creativity, outlined a number of variables that are related to creativity: recognizing patterns in new contexts, making connections and remote associations, taking risks, challenging assumptions, taking advantage of change, and seeing things in a new way. Though Barron was speaking about creativity in a general sense, and about adults, these are all processes that apply to young children in the production of original ideas. It becomes important, then, to recognize the process children go through to come up with ideas. The creative potential of young children may be seen in this creative process as well as in their original ideas or solutions and it is this process that is the precursor to adult creativity. *The process of originality is important to early creative potential.* This developmental concept is portrayed in Figure 2.

In summary, *creativity may be defined as the interpersonal and intrapersonal process by means of which original, high-quality, and genuinely significant products are developed* (Sawyers et al. 1990). This definition considers three different developmental criteria for creativity: originality (for young children), high quality (for older children and adolescents), and genuine significance (by adult societal standards). The next section explains how the characteristics of creative potential may be identified within this developmental perspective.

Figure 2
Developmental Definition

Creativity is the intrapersonal and interpersonal process by means of which

Definition	Process	Criterion	Age
Original (i.e., unusual)	Ideational Fluency	Creative Potential	Preschool
and			
High-Quality (i.e., workable)	Original Solutions	Creative Precursors	School Age
and			
Genuinely Significant (i.e., contributes to society)	Execution of Original Products	Creative Behavior	Adult

products are developed.

DEVELOPMENTAL CHARACTERISTICS
OF CREATIVE POTENTIAL IN YOUNG CHILDREN

The expression of creativity is a developmental process, much the same as other areas of development. Early childhood educators are trained to look for indicators of development in particular areas. In academic areas, for instance, preschool and kindergarten teachers observe a specific set of indicators for prereading skills, while third grade teachers observe a different set of behaviors for third grade reading proficiency. Similarly, preschool children and third graders will express their creativity in different ways. It is important to think of creativity as a developmental process subject to the unique characteristics emerging in each child.

Individual Differences

For young children, creativity is best labeled *creative potential*. As teachers recognize the potential for learning to read by exposing young children to books, so they may also recognize the importance of each child's creative potential for the expression of later creativity.

There is no one profile of a child with creative potential. Inherent in the term *creative* is the idea of uniqueness—thinking, acting, or performing tasks differently. Nor is there one formula for identifying a creative child. C. W. Taylor (1988), whose writings on creativity span 30 years, describes the creative profile of an individual as a "totem pole," where the many "faces" (characteristics or traits) of an individual come together in unique combination to comprise a creative person. Creative potential is seen in many facets of a child's personality and cognitive development and is shaped by biological, cultural, and environmental influences (Sawyers et al. 1990). Moreover, there is an ecological balance in the interaction of individual traits and environmental influences in the development of creative potential and later creative achievement (Harrington 1990;

21

Sawyers et al. 1990).

Environment helps form the profile of the creative child, though we are constantly reminded that "no single set of circumstances give rise to creative works" (John-Steiner 1985, 64). When one reads the biographical works on Thomas Edison (inventor of not only the light bulb, but the phonograph, the alkaline storage battery, the mimeograph, the fluoroscope, and many other devices), one realizes that Edison possessed a unique combination of traits that enabled him to become one of our most famed and productive inventors (Bryan 1926; Jenkins et al. 1989). Yet what stands out in these biographies is the environment that nurtured this kind of thinking. Edison's mother embarked on what is now called "home schooling." This investigative home environment, coupled with Edison's individual characteristics and belief in himself, is thought to have enabled him to reach creative eminence.

In today's schools, the play-based early childhood environment, described in *Developmentally Appropriate Practice* (Bredekamp 1987), *Play in the Lives of Children* (Rogers and Sawyers 1988), and *Play's Place in Public Education for Young Children* (Dimidjian 1991), validates the need for this investigative environment all through the early years. As we begin to understand the characteristics of creative children ages three through eight, then, we must keep in mind that the environment of both the preschool and the primary grades plays an important part in facilitating creative potential.

In the same way, cultural influences must also be recognized. Some cross-cultural research indicates that there are similarities in creativity in young children in the United States and India (Mehrotra and Sawyers 1989) and Israel (Milgram, Moran, Sawyers, and Fu 1987). In these studies, children gave the same proportion of original and popular responses to such queries as, "Name all the things you can think of that are red." Interestingly, research with four-year-olds in Paraguay (Marcos and Moran 1989) found that children gave three times as many popular (uncreative) responses as American children. Paraguayan children were also less likely to elaborate on their responses, giving one-word responses, despite the fact that the test was given in their native tongue. Torrance (1968) reports cross-cultural comparisons among children in 11 cultures. Teachers may be sensitive to cultural differences in response styles among children from different cultures. Likewise, it seems that verbal creativity may be more difficult to recognize in children for whom English is a second language. For these children, teachers should be sensitive to creativity as it may be expressed in many fashions.

The environment influences each child in a slightly different way, depending on the child's unique cognitive and personality traits. In Chapter 3, the role of the environment is discussed in detail. The following pages provide information on how individual cognitive and personality traits of children influence creative potential.[1]

Cognitive Traits

The cognitive characteristics of creative children include fantasy, divergent thinking, metaphoric thinking, conceptual tempo, and curiosity. Teachers are trained to observe children's cognitive development. Often the indicators we notice are those that we can check off or easily quantify (child identifies colors; child counts to 20; child can distinguish between large and small; child can sequence the events of a story). In thinking about creativity, these indicators of cognitive development form the base of

---

[1]Note that much of the information presented in this chapter is based on empirical studies in which children were administered a variety of tests to assess creativity, cognition, personality, intelligence, etc. These references are not meant to indicate that such assessment procedures are appropriate in the early childhood classroom as a means for identifying creative children. Further, creative potential may be observed, recognized, and fostered in the early childhood classroom without formal assessment tools; later chapters discuss this in detail.

knowledge and skills from which teachers may observe the creative process. By looking more globally at the *process of cognition* (how the child arrived at a unique sequence of events for a story) rather than the end *product of cognition* (the actual sequence of events), teachers must begin to ask, "What are the thinking processes that lead to original thinking?"

This section outlines fantasy, divergent thinking, metaphoric thinking, conceptual tempo, and curiosity as processes that contribute to original thinking and that teachers may observe. Observing a process is perhaps more difficult than checking off a skill or a product on a developmental checklist. Take, for example, a group of early childhood teachers participating in a graduate class on curriculum development. These teachers were asked to list examples of how children used divergent thinking (a form of brainstorming) in their classrooms. The teachers' initial response was to list the carefully planned activities in their classrooms where children had completed written assignments (e.g., creative writing) or produced some other tangible evidence of this type of thinking. In other words, the teachers compiled a list of *planned* activities that *produced* divergent thinking. But divergent thinking, like many of the processes listed above (fantasy, curiosity, etc.) cannot always be "planned." Divergent thinking, as explained below, is a process that may be observed during lunch time or free play or during a reading group—it is a *process* not an activity per se. This is an important distinction because as teachers become more adept at observing process, they will also be able to make the link between how children's individual modes of thinking are connected to creative potential.

Fantasy

Creative children engage in more sociodramatic play (Dansky and Silverman 1973; Goodwin, Sawyers, and Barby

1988; Pepler and Ross 1981; Sutton and Smith 1968; Dansky 1980a, 1980b). In fact, understanding the creative potential of young children is so grounded in play that a later section of this monograph is devoted to understanding this relationship. Children who engage in fantasy are likely to be imaginative thinkers. Fantasy activities including imaginative play appear to increase the child's behavioral repertoire and thus stimulate the development of creativity and divergent thinking (Smilansky 1968; Lieberman 1977; Singer 1973). This means that when children engage in fantasy they are learning more about themselves and their environment as well as acquiring knowledge and developing skills that they may use in creative ways. Although not as prevalent in recent years, some preschools and kindergartens with strictly academic goals require children to sit at desks with papers, pencils, dittos, flash cards, and similar materials. Contrast this with children in play-based preschools and kindergartens that encourage and facilitate imaginative play. Which children have experiences that are most likely to stimulate creative potential? It is not surprising when research studies confirm teachers' observations that imaginative play experiences are related to creative thinking in young children (Moran, Sawyers, Fu, and Milgram 1984; Pepler and Ross 1981).

In play-based classrooms, imagination and learning go hand-in-hand. Learning to write may be "taught" using ditto sheets, or writing may be "learned" in a dramatic play situation that uses prescription pads as part of a doctor's office theme. When children engage in fantasy they are free from the influences of evaluation and are more likely to think of unconventional ideas. Along with freedom from evaluation is an atmosphere in which children learn to respect their unconventional ideas and feel good about their imagination.

Fantasy can be seen with young children in situations beyond the dramatic play center. For instance, provide children on the play yard with several large boxes and observe the free flow of fantastic ideas. In a similar vein, ask first graders, "What can you do with an empty shoe?"[2] and observe a similar flow of ideas, beginning with real-life responses and leading to imaginative, fantasy-rich responses. Or how about tapping children's divergent thinking skills by asking them to think of different endings to a favorite story. Think of the many possibilities for expanding Shaw's (1947) classic, *It Looked Like Spilt Milk.* Transfer this way of thinking to real-life problem situations and observe a child who can be guided to retool an imaginative idea into an original, workable solution.

Interestingly, in any classroom a teacher may observe individual differences in children with regard to fantasy. When presented with open-ended activities, some children will almost immediately begin an imaginative monologue of ideas; others will appear confused by the lack of parameters and continue to seek the nonexistent right answer. By recognizing fantasy as a positive indicator of creative potential, teachers can begin to observe children's play, listen to their fantastic stories, and entertain their daydreams through a different set of eyes.

Divergent Thinking

Divergent thinking involves coming up with a variety of responses or ideas. At rest time, some children may show their divergent thinking abilities by presenting several alternatives to taking a nap. For instance, they might suggest quietly looking at books, drawing, doing puzzles, or making a tent out of their cot and sitting quietly (of course) under their new structure. Some teachers may view these ideas as bothersome and manipulative ways of skirting the rules. Other teachers may view them as examples of divergent thinking, even if the nap time rule doesn't change. Another example comes to mind of a first grade boy who composed new verses to every song he learned in school. The

---

[2]B. Stanish. *A Monster's Shoe and the Cat-Kangaroo: A Whole Mind Book for Expanding Creative Potential* (Buffalo: D.O.K. Publishers, 1983).

teacher who recognizes children's attempts to think of alternatives is observing real-life divergent thinking.

Brainstorming is another type of divergent thinking that is more familiar to educators. Brainstorming combines the concepts of nonevaluative acceptance and multiple solutions. When children are encouraged to brainstorm, they come up with many ideas. Techniques to encourage divergent thinking need not be unrelated or just tacked on to an activity. Many daily activities lend themselves to divergent thinking with little modification. For example, teachers often encourage children to explore many different ways to do a book report—written, oral, creating a filmstrip using the overhead projector, or making a videotape.

Humor is related to divergent thinking as a form of "cognitive playfulness" (Ziv 1988). A century ago, Penjon recognized that "laughter is an expression of freedom, freedom from the strict laws of rational thinking and freedom to play with new ideas" (Penjon 1891, 121). Very little research has been done on this topic with young children. Lieberman's classic studies on the relationship of playfulness and creativity with preschool children established a relationship with humor (Lieberman 1965, 1977). In another study, creativity scores and humor were unrelated in young children, though a significant relationship was found after age six (McGhee 1980). Humor, or "cognitive playfulness," may be seen in the form of divergent thinking or in the child who senses cognitive incongruities and thus finds humor in many daily situations. Of course, sensing the incongruities in a situation and making the logical leap from incongruity to humor may require advanced cognitive abilities. Most young children are very literal in their thinking; therefore it is difficult to establish exactly how creativity and humor are empirically related. Yet teachers recognize that the child with a good sense of humor may also be the one who can put the group at ease, remove the threat of criticism from the social environment (Ziv 1988), and help establish a "safe" environment for divergent thinking and problem solving.

Children need to develop both divergent and convergent thinking. The complement of divergent thinking is convergent thinking—thinking converges to a point or to one right answer. Achievement tests, intelligence tests, most phonics or mathematics ditto sheets, and many computer learning games are examples of convergent thinking tasks. When children think of alternative responses on standardized tests, teachers cannot give credit for these answers even when it is apparent that the child knows the concept. So it seems that children will inevitably learn that the "right" answer (though perhaps not the best, most challenging, or creative answer) is the one that is rewarded by high achievement test scores and by unit test scores, yielding "A's" in reading and mathematics.

An exclusive emphasis on convergent thinking can lead to a "right answer orientation" (Treffinger, Isaksen, and Firestien 1982). Such an orientation may be applied to the differences in the behaviors of preschool/kindergarten children and second/third grade children during the administration of creativity tests. Interestingly, researchers (Tegano and Moran 1989) report that when young children were asked to name all the ways to use a box, they were eager to give responses and needed little coaxing. When the same question was asked of older children, however, they often gave one response and then looked questioningly for approval. In other words, "Did I give the right answer?" They seemed to be unaccustomed to and even uncomfortable with these open-ended questions that required divergent responses. Researchers report that after some encouragement and assurance to the children that there are many ways to answer the question, most primary grade children began to generate an imaginative list of responses.

We view divergent and convergent thinking as complementary. In defining creative potential in young children, however, attention to divergent thinking appears more important to the creative process. The freedom to use multiple

28

solutions and original responses forms the base for children's efficient problem-solving skills.

Creativity that involves both originality and products requires both divergent and convergent thinking. Both types of thinking are important to creativity; consequently, the teacher's task is to avoid replacing one with the other. Another way to think about this is that children must learn the rules of a domain (e.g., what are the parts of a book report?) before they can begin to break the rules, change the rules, to be creative (a book report as a board game).

Divergent thinking may decrease as children enter school. It is not unusual to see a decrease in divergent thinking with age. Torrance (1981) reported a "fourth grade slump" in the creativity test scores of children—divergent thinking test scores decrease from preschool to fourth grade. Tegano and Moran (1989) also found that the proportion of original answers given by children on divergent thinking tasks decreased from preschool to third grade. Dudek (1974), following children longitudinally from first through sixth grade, found that "children's creativity begins to dry out early, around age 5; that a serious drop in creativity occurs in grade 4, at age 9, and another in grade 7, at age 12" (p. 83). A group of studies with different age subjects (Milgram et al. 1978; Milgram and Rabkin 1980; Milgram and Arad 1981; Moran et al. 1983) indicated that the proportion of original responses on ideational fluency tasks drops from 50–60 percent in preschoolers to 25–33 percent for elementary and high school students, only to rise again to about 50 percent for young adults.

It is uncertain whether this decrease in divergent thinking is due to the influence of the convergent thinking tasks required in most elementary schools or to normal cognitive and personality development of children or both. These research findings may attest to the effect of socialization and schooling, which makes children and adolescents who spend large amounts of time in a formal school setting more cautious about expressing unusual ideas than either preschool children or young adults whose time is spent in less formal settings. On the other hand, original thinking may be another instance of nonlinear or U-shaped developmental processes similar to those reported by Strauss and his associates (Strauss 1981). This trend may have gone unnoticed because of the paucity of studies with very young children. At any rate, these findings should serve as "red flag" for educators in the primary grades who are concerned with optimizing the creative potential of young children.

Metaphoric Thinking

Recall that Barron (1987) suggested that making connections and remote associations is related to creativity. One expression of that dimension is the ability to produce or comprehend metaphors. When three-year-old Mollie remarks that she "feels like a rainy day," she shows this spontaneous use of metaphor. A review of the research on metaphor and young children suggests several implications for preschool and primary classrooms that warrant the attention of teachers. Suppose you were presented with three pictures: a rundown house, a rat, and moldy cheese, and were asked which pair goes together. (See Figure 3.) Although one might expect to find rats in the old house or eating the cheese, it is the imagery portrayed in the description of the dilapidated house as a piece of molding swiss cheese that provides the metaphor (Kogan, Connor, Gross, and Fava 1980). In studies with school-age children, those who identified and explained a metaphoric relationship were found to have higher scores on divergent thinking tasks—that is, they were able to generate more ideas when presented with a stimulus (Kogan et al. 1980; Malgady 1977, 1981).

Figure 3
Metaphor Task

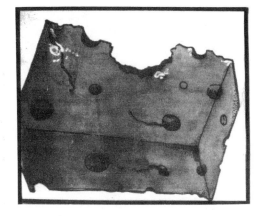

Adapted from "Understanding Visual Metaphor: Developmental and Individual Differences," by N. Kogan, K. Connor, A. Gross, and D. Fava. *Monographs for the Society for Research in Child Development* 45, no. 1 (serial no. 183), 1980.

Metaphor may also be related to intelligence. Successful metaphoric thinking may be dependent on real-world knowledge or general intelligence (Kogan 1983; Vosniadou and Ortony 1983) inasmuch as a child must be familiar with an object and understand its many uses before he or she can form a metaphoric understanding of the object in relation to another object. This idea was confirmed in a study of metaphoric thinking and divergent thinking with preschool children (Sawyers, Moran, Fu, and Horm-Wingerd 1990). In this study the ability to understand metaphors was related to the intelligence of the children. With preschool children we see that metaphor is undifferentiated from intelligence. In the early primary grades metaphor becomes differentiated from intelligence and contributes to the ability for divergent thought.

Metaphors may be observed throughout the day. Early childhood teachers may note instances of metaphoric thought, especially in the play behaviors of children. Take, for example, the child who sees the parallel between the discontented feeling in the classroom after being pent-up inside all day and the unpredictable rustling leaves on a dreary fall day. First, second, and third grade teachers may find more curricular opportunities to observe metaphors as an indicator of creative potential. Although haiku or creative writing are common places for noting metaphors, one astute teacher observed metaphoric thought in a second grader during a mathematics lesson. While constructing and comprehending the concept of simple fractions (cutting pieces of fruit in half and sharing with friends), the child applied the concept metaphorically to another aspect of his life: "I'm like that apple, half of me I share with my family and half of me I share with the kids at school." Like all other indicators of creative potential, metaphoric thinking is not limited to just the "arts" (creative writing or drawing). Metaphoric thinking as an aspect of creativity is a way of perceiving and expressing that may pervade all aspects of a child's life.

Conceptual Tempo

This process generally depicts a cognitive style that determines how a child approaches certain tasks. We all know children who are slow to reach decisions but respond with great accuracy and others who respond quickly but often inaccurately. Kogan (1983) identified the former as "reflective" and the latter as "impulsive." How children approach tasks is important to the process of eliciting divergent thinking. Mednick (1962) believed that a slow, steady rate of responding is more typical of highly creative persons. Though the relationship between cognitive style and creativity has intuitive appeal, the data suggest a much greater complexity.

Impulsive and reflective preschoolers appear quite similar in generating original ideas (Broberg and Moran 1988; Ward 1968). But these studies indicate that *individual differences in the way children approach tasks may have important implications for determining response levels.* Low originality is likely to come from children who are characterized by higher anxiety and a "right answer orientation," as well as by children with low levels of attention to detail, motivation, and perseverance (Broberg and Moran 1988). Some children tend to approach any task as a convergent task with only one right answer, others approach all tasks as divergent, and still others are able to switch response styles to fit the task at hand. The complexity of the relationship between cognitive style and creativity with young children lends itself to future research. For now, it is helpful to recognize that children approach tasks differently and these differences affect their use of divergent or convergent thought.

Curiosity

When any group of educators is asked to describe the creative child, curiosity is one of their first and most important responses. Interestingly, only few investigations of curiosity and creativity have been carried out. Perhaps this is because curiosity, like creativity, is difficult to define and measure. Nonetheless, it seems apparent that these two concepts are inherently related. Teachers observe curiosity daily in children who ask question after question: "What makes the sun shine?" "How can birds fly?" Similarly, when three-year-old Mary Katherine, peering intently into the tape recorder, was asked what she was looking for, she responded matter-of-factly: "I want to know where the guy is who's singing in there."

Curiosity involves exploration. The nonverbal indicators of creativity are perhaps less salient to teachers and may even be misinterpreted as disruptive to the classroom routine. In every group of children there seem to be one or two who are "into everything"—the trees on the playground, the discarded boxes in the hallway, and the custodian's closet full of large buckets and wide dustmops. All these everyday objects are seen as materials to be examined more closely. One teacher reported canvasing garage sales to purchase broken household appliances (old toasters, tape recorders, etc.) and, then, after removing the electrical cords, providing space in the classroom for children to use screwdrivers and pliers to take these "machines" apart, without, of course, ever intending to put them back together.

There is some evidence to confirm that curiosity is related to creativity, at least when creativity is measured as original thinking (or ideational fluency). One study found the exploratory behaviors of kindergarten children to be significantly related to ideational fluency, though the relationship was not as strong for second graders (Cohen 1974). In another study, children who were rated high on curiosity by their teachers also gave more original responses on an ideational fluency task than children who were rated less curious (Inagaki 1979). It seems that the link between creativity and curiosity leads to an understanding of exploratory behavior. That is, children who tend to engage in more exploration are more curious and thus more likely to pose the kinds of questions in play situations that lead to creative problem solving (Griffing et al. 1988; Tegano et al. 1989). Early childhood educators are trained to respect children's curiosity, although recognizing the many faces of curiosity is not always easy.

The traits outlined here, then, provide a picture of the kind of thinking that may lead to creative thinking. These cognitive traits do not appear on teacher checklists, yet they have been shown theoretically and empirically to be linked to creativity in young children. Learning to observe, to recognize, to attend to, and to facilitate these traits is the task of the early childhood educator. The critical first step is becoming a good observer.

Personality Factors

Individual personality traits, like the cognitive traits just discussed, help teachers understand the creative potential of young children. One trait, high self-concept, though not always singled out, is common to most children who exhibit creative potential. This section reviews the personality traits associated with creativity: temperament, conformity, risk-taking, and motivation. These aspects of personality are theoretically and empirically related to creativity, yet, more importantly perhaps, most teachers can immediately identify children they have known and thus make practical connections between theory, research, and classroom examples.

Temperament

Temperament appears to describe relatively stable traits that characterize individual differences in children from birth. There are a number of systems by which to classify temperament, but the most common has been that of Thomas and Chess (1977). These investigators identified nine characteristics of children: adaptability, persistence/attention span, threshold of responsiveness, approach-withdrawal, distractibility, quality of mood, intensity of reaction, activity level, and rhythmicity.

Some evidence exists to link these variables to aspects of creative thought (Bomba and Moran 1989). In this study, distractibility, sensory threshold, and approach were related to original thinking. Children who tended to get more involved with novel objects (approach), who were less distractible (i.e., attended to cues), and who tended to react to low-intensity cues (threshold) generated more responses to ideational fluency tasks. Teachers need to consider the impact of these individual differences in recognizing how children approach tasks and how quickly they can enter into them. Approach can be tied to exploration and curiosity, whereas sensory threshold might account for the findings that show that more creative children use environmental cues more efficiently (Ward 1974). Think of the child in your classroom who seems to notice every detail, then consider the *quality* of the information this child gathers as a positive indicator of creative potential.

Nonconformity

Creativity and nonconformity are generally assumed to be related in some way, but there is little research in this area with young children. Among the few attempts to look at this trait is the work of Starkweather (1971) who pioneered the area of conformity/nonconformity with preschool children in a decade of research in the 1970s. Reasoning that children's freedom of expression was related to creativity, Starkweather developed measures of the motivational characteristics of young children, among them conformity/nonconformity. She clearly believed that "the creative person is willing to be different; he [or she] may conform or not of his [or her] own free will.... [That is to say that] the child who is a compulsive nonconformist is just as rigid as the child who is a compulsive conformist" (1971, 247).

On one of her tests, the Form Boards, a line drawing of a rabbit is shown at the base of a tree. The child was asked to complete the "puzzle" by choosing either a rabbit (conforming) or flowers. In a second session, the line drawing is of the flowers and the child chooses between the rabbit and the flowers. Each child had 80 chances to make choices in the two sessions. In this way, Starkweather was able to distinguish between a child's preference for the rabbit or flowers and the child's conformity.

To measure social conformity, Starkweather determined a child's preference for colors and later asked the child which color he or she would choose to make a booklet for parents or friends, when the parent's favorite color was designated (green, for example). Conforming children chose green to conform to the parent's preference; nonconforming children chose their own favorite color.

These measures of conformity/nonconformity are currently being used with a sample of preschool children in a study of the relationship of impersonal and social conformity to the original thinking of young children (Webb 1991). When completed, this study will help us better understand the role of nonconformity and creative potential in young children.

In another study by Tegano, Bennett, and Pike (1990), teachers rated the degree to which a child is a "nonconformist, does things his or her way." Children with high nonconformity ratings also had high originality scores on a creativity measure. Likewise, high nonconformity ratings by teachers were associated with many of the other personality traits of creative young children discussed here.

Although these studies of young children are few, available research indicates that nonconformity is related to creativity. Most teachers easily remember the nonconformist in their class. Interestingly, the creative nonconformist usually has a high self-concept compared to the compulsive nonconformist who seeks attention by always being different. Sometimes nonconformity may be displayed as behavior problems; in other words, not all nonconforming behaviors are indicators of creative potential. Teachers must make unbiased judgments about interpreting nonconforming behaviors as disruptive; or they may view nonconforming behavior in a more positive light as a personality characteristic associated with creative potential. Especially with preschool and primary children, it is important for both child and teacher to approach nonconforming behaviors with respect.

Risk-Taking

In Starkweather's (1971) work, risking-taking was another motivational characteristic that was conceptualized as "willingness to try the difficult." John-Steiner describes "emotional courage" as an inner resource of the creative individual (1985, 73). Emotional courage is seen in young children who are willing to take a risk, to accept a challenge, to risk making a mistake. One of the invisible tools of scientific thinking may have to do with the willingness to make mistakes (John-Steiner 1985).

> Consider Ryan, a second grader, who, when assigned to write a book report, chose to construct a poem conveying how the book made him feel. This report, with none of the makings of the traditional assignment such as characters or plot, presented his teacher with an interesting dilemma. Ryan took a risk in deviating from the traditional format. How would you respond?[3]

For more information on risk-taking and conformity, see *Risk-Taking in Learning, K-3* (Young 1991).

Motivation

Creativity appears to be guided by an internal locus of control—a process that arises from within the person rather than from external forces (Cohen and Oden 1974). Though there is little research to substantiate this specifically with young

---

[3]Ryan's teacher wrote, "Ryan, you need to turn in your own work." Not only did she not adjust to the nature of the response, she assumed that the poem was not his own.

children, Sawyers and Moran (1984) have found a relationship between ideational fluency and internal control in four-year-olds. This makes good common sense when one thinks of the natural link between children's play and creativity. Both constructs share the criterion of intrinsic motivation; that is, it seems as ridiculous to suggest that we might be able to *force* children to play as it would be to *force* them to think creatively.

In a classroom, the subtle indicators of locus of control may be seen in children who are less likely to seek approval for their actions. In every classroom some children consistently approach the teacher looking for reinforcement: "Guess what, Ms. Smith, I was the one who jumped the most times in P.E." or "Look at my picture, Ms. Smith, what else should I put on it?" This is not to say that all children do not need to seek some approval and that acceptance by teacher and peers is not intricately tied to self-concept. Certainly all children need to feel accepted. Rather, the child who seems to be motivated by external acceptance, at the *expense* of self-appraisal and self-evaluation, is more externally motivated than others. The externally motivated child may be less likely to engage in a creative or open-ended activity because the activity lacks the system of built-in rewards for the right answer. Moreover, it is this externally motivated child who later on may have difficulties moving to the production of a creative product because of the inability for critical self-evaluation.

To begin to engage in creative thinking means being able to set aside the influence of evaluation and to allow ideas to form, change, and combine. Some children seem to be more adept at putting the influence of evaluation aside as they become engrossed in the *process* of thinking, drawing, writing, or calculating in a nonconventional manner. For example:

A third grade teacher has organizational skills as a goal for children. In this classroom two children are very organized. Katie shows indicators of creativity; Rodney does not. Rodney remains concerned about what the teacher thinks; as a result, his organizational skills are his source of praise from the teacher. Katie, although the recipient of the same teacher praise for organization, is less concerned about what the teacher thinks; her organizational skills are internally motivated and become the tools for accomplishing her creative pursuits.

Even as we move to the development of creative products, the motivation for evaluation comes from internal rather than external mechanisms. Only internal motivation could have sustained Edison's testing of filaments for the light bulb before he discovered carbonized cotton sewing thread as the workable solution. Edison's notebooks reveal that he made some 1,600 tests of earth, minerals, and ores in connection with these investigations. In the same vein, he recalls:

> I speak without exaggeration when I say that I have constructed three thousand different theories in connection with the electric light, each one of them reasonable and apparently likely to be true. Yet in two cases only did my experiments prove the truth of my theory. (Edison in Bryan 1926, 125)

It is here that perseverance and critical self-evaluation come into play.

Rewards

Perhaps the most common means of external motivation is the use of rewards, especially material ones. We ask children to eat their broccoli and hold out the apple pie and ice cream as the reward. We place gold stars on the papers of children who answer all their mathematics workbook problems correctly. But what happens when we reward children? Are we encouraging creative thought? By and large, the answer is a resounding no.

The use of tangible rewards appears to adversely affect both motivation and performance. Lepper, Greene, and Nisbett (1973) have shown that if children are rewarded on tasks that

40

they find interesting to begin with, their intrinsic motivation to subsequently engage in such tasks is undermined. As a result, they are less likely to engage in that activity following the reward. McGraw (1978) extended this notion by suggesting that the beneficial effects of rewards are limited to tasks that are either aversive or algorithmic. An algorithmic task is one in which the route to the solution is rather straightforward (i.e., you either know it or you don't). Most creativity tasks would be described as attractive (i.e., intrinsically fun and engaging) and heuristic (i.e., the route to the solution is not clear and, in fact, there are many routes). Indeed, several studies have shown that the quality of creative responses decreases under reward conditions. Children in one of these studies (Groves, Sawyers, and Moran 1987) were given an ideational fluency task and told that "if they did well enough they would receive a prize" which they selected; or they were administered the task under the standard more game-like conditions with no contingent prize. The children who received the promise of the reward averaged only half the number of original responses as did the nonrewarded children, and the rewarded children decreased in response flexibility (the number of categories of responses) as well. There are several theories to explain these findings; they are based on changes either in motivation or in cognitive functioning, which cannot be addressed here. All, however, suggest that tangible rewards appear to be harmful to the creative process.

HOW TO RECOGNIZE CREATIVE POTENTIAL

Intelligence and Creativity

Creativity can be considered within the broad range of intelligent behaviors (Guilford 1956) but it is quite distinct from the type of intelligence commonly measured in school settings (e.g., test performance). How does the more creative child think? Is the child who is first to come up with the correct answer the creative child? Is the child who appears to be daydreaming while

41

considering four or five possible answers the creative child? Is the creative child necessarily an exceptionally bright child?

Consider your adult friends. Do you know someone who is extremely bright, yet perhaps very boring? Do you also know someone who is always coming up with different and fun ideas, though this person may or may not be exceptionally bright in traditional academic areas. Likewise, consider the child who excels in school where the correct answer is rewarded, but who is reluctant to make a decision without first checking with the teacher to make sure it is the "correct" one. Then think of the child who is always suggesting a new or different approach to some classroom activity, or an alternative response to a yes/no question, though this child may or may not be viewed as an exceptional student. In this example, the role of internal motivation, risk-taking, and nonconformity is obvious, while intelligence takes a back seat. A certain amount of intelligence is considered necessary at best, but not sufficient for creativity.

In some cases, teachers may find themselves rewarding the correct answer while inadvertently denying children the opportunity to use their thinking skills to come up with original ideas. One often-used example is the "What's-wrong-with-this-picture?" task. We recall one that shows a giraffe outside a kitchen window. For many people, this is one of the items to be identified as wrong. However, if we lived in Africa or next to a zoo or near the circus grounds, seeing a giraffe in such a location becomes a real possibility. Our first response limits these possibilities. So, too, would we be limited by saying that wearing snow boots inside the house is "wrong," or that hanging a picture on the wall upside down is "wrong" (silly, perhaps, but not wrong). In this type of activity, the items are sometimes classified logically-physically (i.e., defying the natural laws, at least as we know them today) or socioculturally (i.e., going against standard practice). The giraffe, snow boots, and upside-down picture are examples of the latter classification. They are wrong only if we assume the perspective of a certain type of neighborhood or a certain set of social parameters.

Another example is the typical kindergarten worksheet where the child's task is to find similarities in a group of pictures (classification skills). In the first row are a dog, a cat, a canary in a cage, and a coat. The obvious correct answer on this item is that the coat is not an animal. But some child may be thinking, "All the pictures have a kind of fur (fur coat, cat fur, and a furry dog), and only the bird has feathers." Thus the bird appears to be the picture that doesn't fit. Or another way of thinking is that cat, cage, and coat all begin with the letter "C," so dog doesn't fit. Teachers could use this kind of worksheet as an exercise in divergent thinking where the goal is to find the most answers, not the right answer.

Remember that creative potential is not the same as intelligence. In the preceding example, the teacher may have rewarded the child who picked the "right" answers with a good grade, in the same way that the child who picks the "right" answers receives points on an intelligence test. Creative potential may be seen in children of high or low intelligence, but intelligent children are not always likely to think creatively. Wallach (1970) argued strongly for the distinction between creativity and intelligence and demonstrated this independence in a classic study of high school students (Wallach and Wing 1969). Over the past 10 years nearly every study of young children has generally found no correlation between intelligence and creative potential (e.g., Moran, Milgram, Sawyers, and Fu 1983). Knowledge and skill play a part in creative production but apparently not in the creative process that generates original ideas.

Intelligence and Talent

When teachers are not trained to recognize creativity, they often mistake signs of advanced cognitive development or exceptional skills for creativity. A child who exhibits exceptional

43

skills or abilities at an early age is often identified by teachers and parents as creative. The child who displays these advanced capabilities may be talented/gifted but not necessarily highly creative. For example, while a child may have command of a descriptive vocabulary and verbal skills beyond his or her years, the child is not necessarily capable of creating an original or imaginative story that captivates the listener with visual images of high quality. Children with advanced verbal skills are likely to talk more than others; therefore they are often mistaken to be creative.

Likewise, talented children have high skill levels but a high skill level is not necessarily the same as creativity. For example, a second grader may be able to play a sophisticated piece of music on the piano—playing all the correct notes and providing an accurate representation of reality. Yet this performance does not demonstrate creativity—a novel approach or originality. The young musician who varies the score to draw emotive reaction from us and makes us *feel* the music may be the one who is creative. In these cases we confuse the precocious (i.e., unusual verbal skills or talent) with the unusual (i.e., original) in our personal definition of creativity. Of course we may also find children who are indeed gifted, talented, *and* creative.

Research documents teachers' difficulties in recognizing the creative children in their classroom. In one study by Nicholson and Moran (1986), preschool teachers trained in creativity were asked to identify the most creative children in their classrooms. The children were then assessed for intelligence and creative potential using standardized measures. The teachers were generally unsuccessful in identifying the creative children; instead, those they identified as creative were actually the most intelligent children.

Why is it difficult for teachers to identify creative children? Perhaps teacher training has not traditionally empha-sized creativity in the same way that it has emphasized the acquisition of knowledge. Perhaps creativity is simply harder to recognize. Indeed, subtle indicators of creativity may be hard to recognize, especially when they don't lead to creative products. Teachers are not as familiar with creativity tests or theory as they are with tests or theory underlying other cognitive skills. Traditionally, teachers have not been given an adequate knowledge base about what creativity is and how to identify and nurture it in the classroom.

Teacher-Driven Definitions

When teachers defined creativity using the social validation process (Runco 1987), they were more successful. In this process, one group of teachers is asked to describe the creative child. The most frequently occurring descriptions are used to compile a list of characteristics and behaviors of creative children. A second group of teachers uses this list to rate the children in their classes. Then these teachers' ratings are compared to the children's scores on creativity and intelligence tests.

Recently we were successful in distinguishing between creativity and intelligence in preschool-age children using some of Runco's ideas with teachers developing their own conceptions of creativity (Tegano, Bennett, and Pike 1990). In this study, a group of early childhood and elementary teachers attended summer workshops on creativity and education. Later, these teachers were asked to describe the personalities and cognitive traits of the creative children they had taught. The most frequent responses of this group were then given to a different group of preschool teachers who were asked to rate the children in their classrooms. From these ratings, 12 traits were shown to be related to children's scores on a creativity measure and were also distinct from intelligence. Other groups of children have also been rated by their teachers on the 12 traits; those with high ratings gave more original responses on a creativity measure but were not necessarily the most intelligent children. The 12 traits identified by teachers are as follows:

1. risk-taking, willingness to try the difficult
2. sense of humor
3. opinionated, outspoken
4. flexible, accommodates to unexpected changes
5. self-directed, self-motivated
6. interested in many things, curious, questioning
7. engages in deliberate systematic exploration, develops plan
8. makes activities uniquely his or her own, "personalizes" activities
9. imaginative, enjoys fantasy
10. nonconformist, does things his or her way
11. comes up with many solutions to a problem
12. uninhibited, free-wheeling style

These 12 traits, found on the Preschool Creativity Rating Scale (see Appendix), correspond to the cognitive and personality traits described earlier. Traits such as fantasy, divergent thinking, curiosity, nonconformity, humor, and risk-taking are also found on the rating scale. The exceptions are items 8 and 12, which deal with personalizing activities and freewheeling style. These traits are difficult to examine in research studies, yet teachers consistently identified them in children they saw as creative. The rating scale is not meant to be used as a single means of identifying creative preschool children. It may benefit early childhood educators most by making them more *aware* of what to look for when thinking about creative children. Because the social validation process was not successful in identifying creative fifth graders in a study by Miller and Sawyers (1989), this method is still being refined in the research literature.

The Preschool Creativity Rating Scale, then, may be a tool to help teachers become aware of the indicators of creative potential in young children. With such an awareness, teachers

46

may begin to facilitate the development of creative potential in all children in their classrooms. These 12 traits are easily observable as teachers plan curricula to encourage creativity; they are highlighted in a later section of Chapter 3.

SUMMARY

Creativity is a construct that is defined developmentally. For young children, the focus is on the creative process, not the creative product. Within the developmental framework, the correlates of creativity are diverse; thus any one profile of a creative child may differ from the profile of another creative child. No two creative children are alike. Each child possesses a unique combination of cognitive and personality traits that may be observed in their relation to the creative process.

This chapter has provided only sketches of the cognitive and personality traits that have been theoretically and empirically linked to creativity in young children. How the cognitive traits of fantasy, divergent thinking, metaphoric thinking, conceptual tempo, and curiosity, and the personality traits of temperament, nonconformity, risk-taking, and internal motivation come together in any one child may be recognized by teachers as one part of the puzzle in developing creative potential. The remaining parts of the puzzle include the curricula and the teacher in forming a dynamic interactive system of the developing creative child's educational experience. Add to this system the biological, cultural, and family variables and the puzzle becomes more interesting and certainly more challenging. Early childhood educators can influence the creative potential of young children first by understanding the individual cognitive and personality profiles of the children and then by looking closely at our approach to curricula (Chapter 3) and the individual characteristics of teachers (Chapter 4).

Chapter 3

THE CURRICULUM: SETTING THE STAGE FOR CREATIVITY

Conclusion

" Although Dr. Albert Einstein's statement that "imagination is more important than knowledge" might be challenged, it is almost axiomatic that knowledge can be more powerful when creatively applied. (Osborn 1963, 1) "

Creativity is fun. Being creative, feeling creative, experiencing creativity is fun. Learning is fun for more children in classrooms where teachers and children recognize and understand the process of creative thinking. Incorporating creative thinking into all areas of the curriculum contributes to a positive attitude toward learning. As one teacher commented, "I used to think that if children were having *too* much fun they couldn't be learning. Now I understand how they are learning in a more effective way." This chapter addresses the relationship of creativity to curriculum and provides guidelines for encouraging creative thinking throughout the preschool and primary school day.

Creativity is an integral part of each day; it may be seen during circle time, reading time, and lunchtime—it is not limited to creative movement, art, music, science, blocks, or dramatic play. Creativity and curriculum should not be at odds with each other; they should complement each other. Children need knowledge and skills to be creative—that is, the curriculum provides the *what* and this chapter provides the *how*.

Experientially based early childhood curricula are congruent with a play and problem-solving approach. From this perspective, observing the *process* of play and exploration,

48

understanding how the structure of an activity influences the potential for creative thinking, and viewing play and exploration as part of the lifelong process of creative thinking are salient components of teaching.

Throughout this chapter, keep in mind that creative thinking is contagious—from teacher to child, from child to teacher, and also from child to child and teacher to teacher.

THE RELATION OF CREATIVITY AND CURRICULUM

conclusion

Children need knowledge and skills to express their creative potential. "Knowledge and skills are necessary before creative potential can have meaning" (Amabile 1983; Barron 1987). Children cannot develop high-level creative thinking skills without the basic knowledge and skills of a particular domain, in the same way that a great chef must develop culinary skills and possess knowledge of spices and herbs before creating the gourmet recipe. The curriculum is the teacher's choice of what knowledge and skills are important and also developmentally appropriate for a particular group of children (Bredekamp 1987; Katz and Chard 1989). Formal instruction represents the transfer of conventional knowledge. Even a child prodigy must practice to acquire the knowledge and skill to play the piano before making the notes sound uniquely expressive.

An example of the need for a knowledge base emerged in the early pilot testing of a measure of creative potential for young children (Moran et al. 1983). The researchers were trying to adapt the classic "Uses" task for preschool children. In this task, subjects are asked to name all the uses they can think of for a common item; the number of original (i.e., unusual) answers serves as one way to measure creativity (Wallach and Kogan 1965; Torrance 1962). The researchers were puzzled when a group of preschool children could think of only a few uses for common objects such as a clothes hanger and a table knife. The

49

research team realized that the reason for the limited response was that the children had little or no knowledge and skill in the use of clothes hangers and table knives. In fact, most preschool children are not allowed to use these items. Knowledge and skills are a prerequisite for creativity. Subsequent research yielded tasks where children were asked to think of all the ways to use a box and paper, items about which children have a working knowledge (Moran et al. 1983). As Barron (1987) asserts, creativity evolves from a knowledge base—*without knowledge, there is no creation.*

Thus, one role of preschool and primary grade teachers is to provide an adequate base of knowledge and skills for children, while simultaneously providing an environment that facilitates creative thinking in the use of the knowledge and skills. The curriculum is the guide by which teachers determine *what* will be presented to children. Creativity is fostered in the way—or *how* the curriculum is presented to the child.

THE ROLE OF EXPLORATION AND PLAY

An Integral Part of the Curriculum

Let's take a look at a classroom where computers are available and see how teachers may observe the process of exploration as it leads into play. At first the computer is novel and children engage in random punching of keys—exploring what the keys can do. This leads to the eventual realization that specific keys have specific uses. This process of *exploring* the computer to discover what it can do may take several months, depending on the frequency of the child's exposure to the technology. When the child has gained an understanding of what the computer can do, she or he may move on to another question: "What can *I* do with the computer?" Equipped with the skills gained through exploration (using a mouse, for example), the child truly begins to *play* with the computer.

Here again, it is important for the child to have

conventional knowledge of what a computer can do and the skills to operate it. But children also need to explore the computer before formal instruction takes place. Then, after they have acquired knowledge and skills, they can use the computer creatively.

Play provides a flexible atmosphere that encourages creative thought. The role of exploration and play is central to understanding how preschool and primary grade children gather and construct information and solve problems.

A parent has just donated 10 dozen very long thin balloons (the kind that clowns fashion into animals) to a second grade class. These unusual balloons are a new experience for most of the children. They immediately begin to examine them. The balloons are long. They are thin. They are of many colors. They are only partially blown up, with four inches unblown at the end of each balloon. Then the children begin to twist the balloons. They squeak. One twist comes loose, three twists stay tight. With every twist the unblown end-piece grows shorter.

The children are exploring the properties of this novel material. They are asking themselves questions: "What can these balloons do?" "What are the properties of these balloons?" Hutt (1979) calls this phase *specific exploration*. The experience in the second grade class continues:

Some children begin to twist the two ends together to form a ring. They embellish the ring with another balloon and it becomes a hat. They twist several balloons together to form a starburst. Other children are making various animals and one boy makes a catcher's mask to wear on his head.

These second graders have gone beyond the initial question, "What can these *balloons* do?" to the next question,

51

"What can *I* do with these balloons?" Hutt (1979) calls this phase *diversive exploration,* but it is more commonly called *play.*[4]

The outcome of this activity was a cooperative creation. The children combined all their individual sculptures into one very long train-like balloon sculpture, paraded it onto the playground and past the principal's office (for pictures), and then named it the "Bubblegum Rainbow."

What was important here was not the product, especially since the product was unknown at the beginning of the activity and would eventually deflate and be thrown away. Rather the teacher was observing the *process of exploration and play* that eventually produced a series of problems: "What can I make with these balloons?" "What will happen if I combine two or more balloons?" "What do I do when I don't have enough balloons?" "What might happen if we combine all the balloons?" The process of exploration and play is an integral part of a curriculum that facilitates creative potential.

Keep in mind that with development, the product becomes more important. Indeed, even by second grade, a child may have developed limited skills to make a product.

Extended periods of exploration will be observed only with truly novel or unusual materials or ideas. With maturity, shorter periods of exploration are needed to deal with the environment. The balloon example illustrates a highly *un*structured activity. As might be expected, all the children did not immediately begin to explore the balloons with the same degree of interest (i.e., each child had a different profile of curiosity and internal motivation). Thus the teacher became a facilitator, asking questions to spark the interest of the less motivated children: "What would happen if you twisted the balloon?"

---

[4]Hutt (1979) proposed that children are asking themselves one of two questions: "What can this object (idea) do?" indicating the *exploration* phase; or "What can I do with this object (idea)?" indicating what we call the *play* phase.

"Does it react differently when it is twisted near the top or near the bottom?" or "How could you make your balloon look like John's?"[5] In this way, the teacher added an element of structure to the activity that was necessary for a particular child to continue in the exploration phase.

Using a Structure Continuum

The Structure Continuum (Figure 4) may serve as a guide for understanding the structure level of a given activity and as a means of evaluating the potential for creative thinking inherent in the activity (Tegano et al. 1989). The balloon activity was a highly *un*structured activity, in which the nature of the product could not be anticipated. This is similar to presenting playdough to a child with no other props. At first, the child may not make anything with the playdough and then make a snake, a ring, a house, or a person. When we add props to the playdough, we add an element of structure to the activity. For instance, with the addition of toothpicks, the activity invites "poking" the playdough (moderately *un*structured). When rolling pins, cookie cutters, or other more structured items are added, the props have shaped the expected outcome and the activity becomes moderately structured. When the teacher sits down at the table and shows the children what to make or provides pizza hats and pizza boxes, the activity becomes highly structured because the outcomes are predetermined.

The level of structure of an activity, then, is a function of the degree to which the materials and activity suggest the outcome. Consider the difference between a moderately *un*structured and a moderately structured activity in a kindergarten. In the first type of activity, toothpicks and bendable straws were on the playdough table. These props suggested no specific products

---

[5]These questions are similar to those proposed by Kamii (1978) as guides for teachers planning physical knowledge activities.

Figure 4

Structure Continuum: Teacher's Planned Level of Structure
and Child's Level of Structure

I wonder what the children would do if I put pipe cleaners with the playdough.

What should I plan for this center today? The children will make zoo animals from playdough.

1	2	3	4
MATERIAL ONLY	**MATERIAL + UNSTRUC-TURED PROPS**	**MATERIAL + STRUCTURED PROPS**	**MATERIAL + MODEL OR INSTRUCTIONS**
Material with no additional props	Props that do not suggest specific purpose	Any combination of props with at least one structured prop	Teacher instructions or a model displayed at center
Playdough only	Toothpicks Straws Beads Pipe cleaners	Cookie Cutters Molds Presses	Bakery sign Model of Snowman
Blocks only	Carpet Squares Scarfs Bedsheets Ropes	Farm animals Cars and trucks Airplanes	Wrapping paper and tape with instructions to play birthday party Airport with preconstructed runways

to the children. They began to interact with the toothpicks and straws in an intensive period of exploration and curious children asked, "What can these straws and toothpicks do with this playdough?" Exploration was followed by a period of extended play as everything from birthday cakes to rocket ships emerged. But several days later, when cupcake tins (moderately structured) were put on the playdough table, the children immediately began playing at making cupcakes and the period of exploration was minimized.

Although in free-play situations, the structure of an activity may easily be observed and altered, it is just as appropriate to examine the structure level of more "academic" activities. For example, in a third grade classroom map skills may be learned from the text or in various configurations of a treasure hunt activity. A treasure hunt encourages children to explore the map of the room and to solve the problems presented by the teacher (e.g., "X" marks the spot). However, some children may alter the structure of the activity by defining their own problems and creating their own maps to share with classmates. Exploration and play are integral parts of this process.

Relating this to the process of creative thinking, teachers watch curious children enter the phase of exploration, thus becoming aware of individual differences in the amount of exploration found in any group of children. Teachers also develop an awareness of how to facilitate creative thinking in play by restructuring activities to invite investigation by even the less curious.

Developmental differences between ages three and eight must also be taken into consideration in structuring activities. Older children may be more concerned with the "right" way, the "adult" way of doing something, so that knowledge and skills take on a special importance to the primary-age children. In structuring activities, however, it is important to remember that exploration with materials or ideas precedes formal instruction. Then, knowledge and skills are introduced in a way that enables children to truly construct meaningful information. Once children are armed with knowledge and skills, they may engage in the process of playing with and changing these materials and ideas.

No Clear-Cut Transition
from Exploration to Play

A child may alternate for some time between the two phases, although initially specific exploration precedes play. This was the case with the toothpicks, straws, and playdough. The children explored the materials and then began the process of construction. Midway through construction, problems arose, sending the children back to the exploration phase to gather information about the properties of the materials to be used in solving the problems. For instance, in the playdough example as Justin was making a unique "spiny turtle," he realized that the playdough was stuck inside the straws. Subsequently, several moments were devoted to figuring out how to get the playdough out of the straws. Several children were invited to help in this very serious endeavor. Finally two solutions were tested successfully—blow it out and squeeze it out. Both produced wonderful round worm-like objects that were then incorporated in the play. The learning taking place at this playdough table is distinctly different from that at the table with the playdough and the same cookie cutters day after day.

Altering the Structure Level

When children are not using a particular material or an activity has become repetitious, teachers can use the continuum in Figure 4 to renew interest and learning. They can further structure an activity by adding a rolling pin to the playdough, for example, to increase the potential for problem finding. Or they might best facilitate problem finding by removing the rolling pin, thereby encouraging the child to come up with another way to roll out the playdough. Or in the treasure hunt example, a set of new markers, rulers, and templates may increase the intrigue of mapmaking for older children; not to mention what might happen if the parameters of the treasure hunt were extended to the entire school building or the outdoor school grounds. We know that new materials, the type of task, and the difficulty of the task are related to the intensity of the play and problem solving (Vandenberg 1980). Teachers who develop a feeling for the degree of structure of an activity can begin to consciously encourage children to discover their own problems.

The Play and Problem-Solving Model: Building a Bird's Nest

The Play and Problem-Solving Model (Figure 5) demonstrates how exploration and play promote opportunities for creative problem solving. Consider the many educationally relevant problems that may occur in a preschool or primary classroom that are solved by teachers rather than by children. The model may be applied when children discover ants in the classroom (figuring out what attracts them, what kind they are, and how to get rid of them, for example). What about other problems: recycling, too much noise in the cafeteria, or creating a bulletin board for open house? Additional information about this model may be found in Tegano et al. (1989), but a few ideas are highlighted here.

Identify the problem: How to build a bird's nest. Consider a group of first graders learning about birds. After exploring and playing with several birds' nests, eggs, feathers, books, and pictures of birds at the discovery center, several children decide they would like to build a bird's nest. Applying this scenario to the Play and Problem-Solving Model, the children have discovered a problem. The center was constructed for discovery of problems (e.g., with books about birds), rather than for

Figure 5
Play and Problem-Solving Model

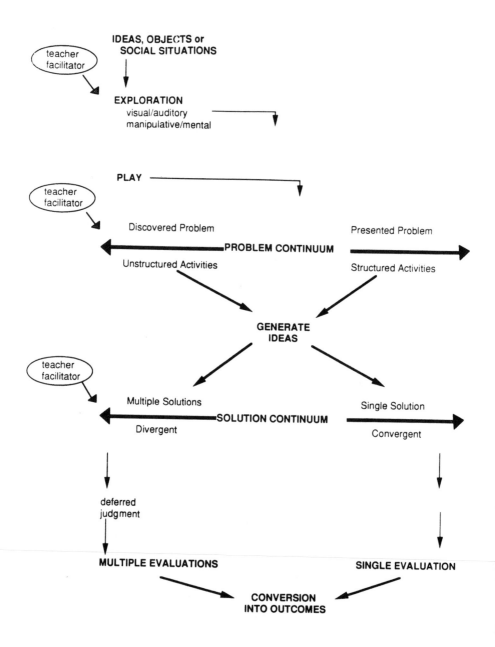

convergent thinking (e.g., with dittos of bird activities or pre-cut art activities).

Generate a list of ideas or solutions. While outside, the children gather the materials for their nests (straw, grass, twigs, dandelion stems) and return to the classroom to begin construction. Another problem obviously arises when they realize that there is no way to make the materials stay together. One child suggests using glue, but this idea is not well received by the "purists" of the group. Thus, the teacher steps in to facilitate a non-evaluative brainstorming session, writing all the ideas for adhesive materials on the board. *Judgment is deferred* until all ideas are exhausted. Then from this list of ideas, the children begin to gather additional materials (mud, needles and thread, yarn, playdough) and the problem-solving process continues into several workable birds' nests.

Avoid judging ideas and solutions too soon. In this situation, it was critical that the children be given an opportunity to think of many solutions without the threat of immediate evaluation. Generating a list of solutions provides the opportunity for "associative fluency" to kick in. Associative fluency (Guilford 1956) is operating when one idea seems to lead to the next idea and then to the next idea and so on. Evaluating ideas during this phase is the best way to *stop* this process. Imagine children thinking of many ways to end a story the class is writing, while the teacher is giving her approval or disapproval of each idea as it is expressed. The children quickly figure out the teacher's hidden agenda and begin to tailor their responses according the anticipated evaluation. Creative thinking has stopped.

Research has shown that the child who can generate many ideas or solutions is also the one who is most likely to come up with original ideas. The more creative ideas usually come near the end of the session; the less creative ones come first (Mednick 1962; Moran et al. 1983). That is, *more ideas* may bring *better (more original) ideas.* Pellegrini (1984) found that exploration and play increased preschool children's associative fluency; in our example, extended exploration may increase the number of ways to build a bird's nest. Interestingly, several varieties of birds' nest emerged from this process, some more sturdy and authentic than others, some totally original.

Evaluation completes the process. Although in this first grade classroom there was no formal evaluation of the bird nests, it was apparent that some nests were "better constructed" than others. With young children, the process of evaluation may appear unplanned and may take the form of trial and error. With older children, the process becomes more important. As children get older and become interested in converting ideas into outcomes, they develop skills in systematic thinking that are necessary for evaluation. During the evaluation phase older children refine their skills in convergent thinking. With younger children, the evaluation process is perhaps less sophisticated but still an integral part of the problem-solving process.

OTHER WAYS TO ORGANIZE
CLASSROOM ACTIVITIES FOR CREATIVITY

The optimal development of creative potential is best accomplished by looking at the complex interactions of all components of the classroom. There are at least three ways to look at structure and creativity:

- *Teacher Planning:* The teacher determines one kind of structure in planning the activity (open-ended vs. right-answer activities).

- *Interactions of Child:* Each child may restructure the activity by approaching it with a unique style.

- *Interactions with Teacher (or with Other Children):* The teacher may again influence the structure of the activity by the nature and quality of the involvement or interaction (Tegano et al. 1989). In the same way that teachers plan an activity, they also continue to guide the activity. Other children often fill this role as well.

These three kinds of structure are naturally interrelated as they influence the facilitation of creative potential. Thus, in many cases, regardless of what materials comprise an activity, it is the individual characteristics of children and teacher (and other children) that also affect the potential for creativity.

Structure in Materials

Structure in materials and planning of activities is a very simple yet powerful part of the preschool and primary grade curriculum. One director of a university lab school discussed her frustration in trying to convince the teachers that putting out crayons and blank paper was a worthwhile activity. The teachers, apparently believing this was not enough, felt compelled to use cutouts of carrots or vegetables they had prepared at home. Perhaps they thought the director was evaluating their performance, so they needed to use activities that showed teacher-imposed structure rather than child-imposed structure. On the other hand, another teacher was pleased to find that his first graders could keep a daily journal, where the level of structure in teacher planning was low—20 sheets of plain white paper stapled between a construction paper cover with instructions to spend the next 20 minutes writing and drawing about things that were important to the children.

One widely held belief is that highly structured toys inhibit pretend play and creativity. The relationship of structure and creativity, however, is complex and seems to be related to the age of the children (Johnson, Ershler, and Bell 1980; McLoyd 1983; Olszewski and Fuson 1982; Pulaski 1970). In general, high-structure toys may be more likely to elicit creative play in three-year-olds; low-structure toys are more likely to elicit creative play in older children. These results are influenced by the development of symbolic thought throughout childhood (Piaget 1962). In other words, because symbolic thinking is less developed in younger children, they may need more realistic props to engage in dramatic play; while five-year-olds have developed a repertoire of symbols and they may assimilate low-structure toys more easily (Rogers and Sawyers 1988). For example, with three-year-olds we may find that a telephone that looks like a telephone helps to engage them in dramatic play, but with kindergartners a banana or a block as a telephone receiver will be just as likely to spur dramatic play. Kindergarten and first grade children are more capable of making role and prop substitutions in play.

This principle may be applied to many academic settings. When new materials, concepts, or skills are introduced, the structure may need to be flexible, with lower expectation for success (product), and as few "rules"as possible. Such flexibility provides a psychologically safe atmosphere in which exploration and play with new materials, concepts, or skills can augment the learning process. Take, for example, the process of learning to write. Preschool and kindergarten writing centers provide a variety of interesting materials for exploring this process (colored pencils, fat and skinny pencils, crayons, markers, and paper of different sizes, textures, and colors). Paper without lines is introduced first. Then, as children develop control in using pencils, structure is introduced by adding lined paper.

Children may alter the structure level without teacher intervention. In one preschool, four-year-old Robert was using the electric keyboard. The teacher had color-coded the keys to match the colored notes in the songbook—a fairly structured activity. Three-year-old Ashleigh watched intently as Robert methodically matched colors from the songbook to the keys to reproduce recognizable tunes. Ashleigh was engaged in an intense exploration of what this piano keyboard could do by watching Robert's actions. When Robert finished, Ashleigh quickly slid into place and tried to play the keyboard as she had seen Robert do; except at age three, she did not have the skills necessary to make the songs. After several attempts she became unhappy with the activity. Rather than quit or seek adult help, Ashleigh found paper and red, black, and green markers and began to create her own score of music with these three colors. She happily pressed the keys of the three colors and created song after song, none of which sounded like a familiar melody. Her smile was an easily observed indicator of a self-confident little girl who had restructured the situation to meet her developmental level and consequently solved her own problem. Opportunities for this kind of flexibility abound in many classrooms.

A research project was designed to document how individual differences in children are related to structure (Moran, Sawyers, and Moore 1988). In this study, half of the preschool children were given a set of lego pieces (*unstructured materials*); the other half were given the same pieces, as well as a set of wheels (*structured materials*). The two groups were further divided with one half of the children in each group receiving *unstructured directions* to "make things with these legos" and the other half receiving *structured directions* showing them how to make a truck and asking them to make things with the legos. The study indicated that structured materials led to less flexibility in thinking and that this effect was heightened when combined with structured directions. The children in the more structured situation gave less divergent responses. Thus it appears in some ways that "less is better." The structured materials were simply the addition of wheels; the structured directions in this case were little more than demonstration with modeling. Yet the demonstration and materials appeared to limit the children's ability to shift thought from category to category—to engage in broad-based divergent thinking.

Novel and/or unstructured materials already exist in most classrooms. Seeing the potential in these materials for developing children's creativity just takes a second look. For example, children who have learned to take rubbings (e.g., rubbing crayons on paper over a penny) may begin to take rubbings of many classroom and outdoor materials and surfaces spontaneously. When these rubbings are labeled and displayed, children have an additional opportunity to reflect on the activity (child-initiated classification systems may be a logical by-product—things with fine textures compared to things that made big bumps).

Children Restructure Activities

Each child structures an activity in an individual way. Chapter 2 delineated the parameters of individual differences (cognitive and personality) that are thought to be related to creativity. As teachers, our job is to become keen observers of how each child interacts with materials, with peers, and with teachers, and then to consider this information along with our knowledge of creativity. In the writing center example, the developmental level of readiness for writing would be easily observed by watching how each child chose to structure her or his interactions with the materials in the center. Some kindergarten children will have difficulty forming the first letter of their names while others will pick out the computer paper to write their names on the lines.

Teachers Restructure Activities

Teachers interact with children to change the structure of activities. In the normal flow of any school day, teachers communicate with children in nondirective/directive and facilitative/evaluative ways. Likewise, teachers observe the influence of peers on children. The influence of these kinds of interactions on the creative process is discussed in more detail in Chapter 4.

FEELING TRAPPED BY
TEXTBOOKS AND CURRICULA

For some early childhood educators, the idea of teaching in ways that promote creativity seems at odds with what is laid out in textbooks and curriculum guides. Indeed the goal of some textbooks is to provide such directions to teachers in terms of "what to say and when" that the materials are often classified as "teacher-proof." Within the model that we see as necessary for developing creativity and problem solving, teachers need to be *empowered* to interact with the child and the materials. These teachers assume responsibility for enabling children to cycle through exploration and play through observation and facilitation. To do this, learning objectives must be reformed to concentrate on concepts and long-term progress rather than on acquisition of small bits of knowledge.

Furthermore, the pressure for high test scores often leaves teachers feeling trapped by a school system's adopted textbook series and approved curriculum. This has recently become a critical issue, especially in early childhood education.

> Achievement tests . . . narrowly emphasize one area of a child's development, the intellectual, and that in a fragmented and narrowly defined way. The tests' narrow "academic" emphasis, in turn, encourages teachers to focus on narrowly defined, isolated "skills," and to spend disproportionate amounts of time on activities that promote the learning of these skills. This often comes at the expense of other aspects of children's development—social, emotional, creative, and physical, for example—as activities that promote these aspects are often left out for a lack of time. (Chaille and Barber 1990, 74)

Most teachers have felt the pressure at one time or other to use an established curriculum. It is especially difficult when a teacher sees a "better" way of presenting a lesson. However, many school systems' curricula and textbooks are not in direct opposition to what teachers know are developmentally appropriate knowledge and skills for the children in their classrooms. At the same time, early childhood professionals should also be making their own critical and scholarly evaluations of what *is* developmentally appropriate for a particular grade level (Kamii 1982). In this way teachers may become adept at designing classroom activities that facilitate the creative potential of children while simultaneously helping them construct the knowledge and develop the skills outlined in the curriculum. Textbooks may aid in this process but, again, the manner in which the teacher uses the textbooks may augment the development of creative potential or it may destroy it. The question is not so much about *what* is going to be taught but *how* it will be presented to children to foster creative thinking.

Modifying Curricula

Be willing to change the recipe. Curriculum may be viewed as an outline of knowledge and skills to be learned, rather than a recipe for how they must be taught. The term "learn" implies that exploration and play are part of the process; the term "recipe" denotes a careful following of steps in a specific order and amount to yield a precise product. Analogous to this is a "teaching paradigm," where the lesson is planned, statement by statement. As we know, children are not all the same, so differing amounts and various orderings of ingredients are necessary for each child. Each one may learn the same knowledge and skills in a unique way; therefore the recipe is continually modified. Keep in mind that developmental needs serve as a guide to the sequence in which concepts are introduced.

Consider these questions when modifying curricula to encourage creative thinking:

1. Is the content/concept developmentally appropriate? Is the concept appropriate for pre-operational or concrete operational children? Will the learning allow

66

the children to be both physically and mentally active, to be engaged in active rather than passive activities? (Bredekamp 1987)

2. Are the children intrinsically interested in the content? Is the content "relevant, engaging, and meaningful to the children themselves?" (Bredekamp 1987, 64). Are they actively involved in choosing the materials? (Amabile 1983)

3. Are materials provided for the children to explore and think about? (Bredekamp 1987) Are the materials ambiguous? What is the level of structure of the activity? How can the structure of the activity be modified to meet the needs of individual children? (Tegano et al. 1989)

4. Does the suggested method of teaching provide opportunities for divergent thinking? Is adequate time planned for exploration and play? (Tegano and Burdette 1991; Tegano, May, Lookabaugh, and Burdette 1991). Does the activity encourage children to be curious? (Griffing, Clark, and Johnson 1988) Does the activity allow playful, fantasy-oriented engagement? Does the activity provide opportunities for children to take the initiative? Are there opportunities for children to recycle through the exploration-play-exploration-play sequence? Are the children likely to develop confidence in their ability to find and solve problems?

5. Are there opportunities for children to interact and communicate with other children and adults? Is there an atmosphere of acceptance by other children and adults? Are judgment and evaluation deferred so that ideas have time to be stretched, combined, and embellished? (Parnes et al. 1977; Treffinger 1975).

"Lucy's Project"

In this example of modifying curriculum, Lucy is a motivated, enthusiastic teacher with 10 years experience in early childhood education. Her interest in creativity and early education was sparked by a graduate curriculum class. In pursuit of this interest she designed a project with the goal of "developing ideas for use in my primary classroom that will encourage and enhance children's creative thinking." Lucy explained that she considered building children's self-confidence a top priority. She was convinced that by developing teaching ideas to encourage creative development she could also develop teaching methods that foster children's positive self-concept. In her words:

> Children need to be able to generate or create ideas and feel free to express them without feeling insecure about their worth. My role as the facilitator will not only be to encourage thinking skills and to build confidence but also to develop in the children a sense of respect for others and their ideas. Hopefully, the children will also learn to encourage and nurture each other in the creative process.

Lucy seemed to understand, almost intuitively, that creativity, like self-concept, is an attitude that cannot be separated out of the curriculum into "Creativity Time" or a "Creativity Center." Even though this chapter has presented ideas for using a structure continuum to look at the potential for creative thinking and problem solving, guidelines for providing time for exploration and play, and parameters for deferring judgment of ideas, the classroom examples have come from *all* areas of the curriculum.

The term "integrated curriculum" is often used to mean teaching the same topic in all disciplines throughout the day. It might also mean being cognizant of how we may integrate concepts across all domains of development in any particular discipline. Creativity is similar to this latter version of integration in that we become less centered on the subject matter and more concerned with how the child interacts with the subject matter—cognitively, affectively, and physically. Thinking about Lucy's goal of encouraging creative thinking, we can see that she understood that creativity is an integrated process to be observed and facilitated throughout the day, not a process that is separate from all the other aspects of the child's experiences.

The curriculum provides the subject matter. Modifying the curriculum to encourage creative thinking becomes the common-sense process of altering the recipe to meet the individual needs of each child for creative expression. This approach to teaching is not new. It is the way many of us teach everyday.

Let us return to Lucy's classroom and look at how she modified the curriculum to encourage creative thinking. Lucy set up her own criteria for assessing her activities:

- *Are the children enthusiastic about the activity?* In this way she addressed the children's interest level— intrinsic motivation.
- *Do the children put time and effort into what they do?* Here she was checking on the amount of time allotted for the activity as well as differences in children's task persistence. Daily schedules become helpful and flexible guidelines for planning rather than self-contained determinants of curriculum decisions.
- *Are the children becoming more fluent and original in their ideas?* Lucy knew she must pay attention to the individual thought processes of the children and in doing so she must try to defer judgment of ideas during the divergent thinking process.
- *Do the children feel good about what they have done? Are they proud of their finished product?* This is basic for Lucy. Here she was able to help children develop a sense of respect for their ideas and for the ideas of other

69

children—"to encourage and nurture each other in the creative process." Keep in mind that all creative endeavors, especially with young children, may not have a product.

Lucy's next step was to take a lesson from her unit on dinosaurs and modify it to meet her criteria. The lesson and evaluation follow.

Dinosaur Models

Activity: Create dinosaurs by gluing boxes together and spray paint them. Decorate with other materials.

Learning: Divergent thinking skills, problem solving, fine motor skills, spatial relations, aesthetic appreciation.

Materials: Boxes of different sizes (no larger than shoe boxes), construction paper, glue, markers, paint, paper plates, toilet paper rolls.

Observations and Reactions of Children: Children had fun but had a hard time developing their own ideas of how to put on spikes, scales, eyes, etc., or even what to put on dinosaurs. I had to give more suggestions and help than I really like to do. Children liked the activity and were proud of what they had done.

Comments: Next time I need to have more discussion and generate more ideas on how and what to put on the dinosaurs—present more options, let children give ideas.

Clearly, Lucy realized that the children did not have the knowledge and skills to optimize the creative potential of this activity (e.g., the fine motor skills to cut and fold paper, to attach three-dimensional objects to each other or to the parts of a dinosaur). Even though the lesson did not meet Lucy's expectations, it did integrate all areas of the child's abilities in the process of creation (fine motor skills in cutting and manipulating materials; cognitive skills in identifying and solving problems throughout the lesson; and affective skills in the sense of pride in accomplishment). Although Lucy was essentially accurate in her comments that she had given options for the materials used by the child, the activity was highly structured with fairly set goals (i.e., depiction of a dinosaur). Rather than using dinosaurs, teachers could decrease the structure by having children conceive of and build a monster, with no preconceived notion of the finished product.

Let's look at another one of Lucy's lessons later in the spring. For this language arts activity, Lucy used one of her favorite books, *The Bugs, the Goats, and the Little Pink Pigs* (by Bill Martin, Jr., and John Archambault, DLM Teaching Resources, Allen, Texas, 1987), modifying the activity to encourage more creative thinking.

The Bugs, the Goats, and the Little Pink Pigs

Activity: Read and sing this book several times over a period of several days. When children are familiar with it, have them write their own verses and draw pictures. Put these together as a book and sing with the class. Example from pages 1 and 2 (in original book):

"WE CAN (read)," SAID THE LITTLE (green bugs).

AND THEY (read) ALL (night) BY THE (light of the moon).

Learning: Sequence of story, divergent thinking, writing skills, fine motor skills.

Materials: Big flip book *The Bugs, the Goats, and the Little Pink Pigs,* paper, tape, or other fastener.

Observations or Reactions of Children: Children loved this book/song. They giggled through it and wanted to hear it over and over. They were very motivated to write their own verses—some were more creative and original than others; a few copied neighbors.

Comments: I might consider writing pages 1 and 2 at separate times. It seemed that more effort and thought were put into page 1. Page 2 ideas may have been quick responses.

This is a good example of how a tried and true activity can be made even better. In essence, Lucy read one of her favorite children's books and then extended the activity across several days so that the children could become familiar with the sequence and organization of the book (i.e., learning the *sequence and organization* are the *skills and knowledge* that are needed in this activity so that it may be extended to creative thinking). She found that children were able to fill in the blanks with their own ideas, though perhaps two pages were too much for one day. What might have happened if the writing activity had been repeated for several more days and children were encouraged to think of new and different ways to fill in the blanks and create new verses? Perhaps more original ideas might have emerged. While some children would have continued to be challenged by the activity, others might have lost interest. A new book with a similar format could be used or perhaps the newly created verse could be dramatized.

Lucy's project was designed to help her recognize ways to facilitate creative thinking; it included ten activities across a six-week period. With each activity, Lucy became more aware of the process of creative thinking. Among the comments in her self-evaluation of this project were references to her role in recognizing and encouraging creative thinking in the children in her classroom. She explained that she had developed a greater awareness of her role as a facilitator in this process, adding:

> This project has been very motivational. Concentration on creative activities during the past few weeks has given mutual enjoyment to both children and teacher. I find myself more frequently assessing activities for possibilities of how I might present them in a creative or problem-solving way. These few weeks have been a good start on creative planning.

Lucy realized that creativity is an atmosphere that pervades the classroom and many opportunities exist throughout the day for encouraging creative thinking. Even the slightest alteration in the teacher's approach to an activity can produce occasions for learning when children generate their own ideas and problems and construct new knowledge on their own terms.

RESEARCH ON CREATIVITY
AND SCHOOLS

Creativity is a trait that fosters problem-solving skills, skills needed in our complex world. Research on model programs has addressed creativity. A few studies compared didactic preschool models to discovery models, where creativity was assessed directly, or more often, observed as curiosity or inventiveness (Dreyer and Rigler 1969; Meizitis 1971; Miller and Dyer 1975; Schweinhart, Weikart, and Larner 1986). Although the findings are confused by methodological differences in the studies, the general conclusions support the discovery model in fostering children's creativity. Perhaps this is because the "discovery" or "open" classroom most closely matches the psychologically safe environment that is essential to develop creative potential.

Preschool Models:
Didactic vs. Discovery

The High/Scope Educational Research Foundation studied the consequences of three preschool curriculum models through age 15: High/Scope (based on Piagetian theory), DISTAR (based on theories of behaviorism), and a model in the nursery school tradition. Schweinhart, Weikart, and Larner report:

> Young children appear to learn from both their relationship to the teacher and peers and the manner in which knowledge is gained.... The latest interpretation from the study, tenuous though the data are, now must be that a high-quality preschool curriculum is based on *child-initiated learning activities.* (1986, 42–43)

73

This conclusion is in accordance with our understanding of how the child and the curriculum interface for optimal creative development. Child-initiated learning implies internal motivation; high interest, relevant content; freedom to change or alter an activity; and an atmosphere of acceptance of children's ideas.

In the primary grades, the open classroom approach of the 1960s and 1970s was seen by many educators as an unsuccessful attempt at experiential, individualized learning. These schools without walls, though theoretically sound, were often created by school districts without providing proper training for teachers. In most cases, the "new" approach was imposed on teachers who had little or no understanding of the philosophy behind it. Although the walls were torn down, the teachers continued to teach in the traditional fashion, but in a noisy and chaotic atmosphere. Sadly, even teachers who wished to change often found they were not able to do so effectively—changes are more effective when they occur gradually and with understanding and commitment (Hennessey and Amabile 1987).

There are many similarities between today's play-based, experiential, developmentally appropriate classrooms and the open classroom approach. What are the similarities? How can we avoid making the same mistakes? Most educators would agree that effective classrooms are characterized by environments in which children are intrinsically motivated to learn (Hennessey and Amabile 1987). Inherent in the concept of intrinsic motivation is the issue of children's perceptions of control. Children who perceive a psychologically safe classroom environment are those who are most likely to develop and learn to express their creativity. In today's vernacular, a play-based, experientially focused classroom with a warm, supportive teacher empowers children to be curious, to inquire, to experiment, and to think for themselves.

It is also important to acknowledge that *all* open classrooms were *not* unsuccessful. In a synthesis of 153 research studies, children in open classrooms were found to have an advantage in their attitude toward school and teachers, curiosity, general mental ability, cooperativeness, creativity and independence; there were no differences for these children in such variables as achievement, locus of control, self-concept, and anxiety (Hedges, Giaconia, and Gage 1981; Walberg 1984).

The goals of open education included the presence of a diverse set of materials to explore; process orientation to learning; children active in guiding their learning; an integrated approach to curriculum; heterogeneous grouping of children; teaching style based on the needs of individual children rather than specified in advance by curriculum materials; diagnostic evaluation style rather than comparing children to the norm; team teaching; flexible use of classroom space (Giaconia and Hedges 1982; Henderson 1975). These goals closely parallel the orientation of most effective early childhood programs today. Hennessey and Amabile conclude:

> Future studies must look specifically at the element in open education that researchers . . . have linked to increases in intrinsic motivation and creative performance—elements that allow students to take control of the learning experience. Present findings lead us to conclude that the amount of freedom children experience in the classroom has an impact on their creative ability. Much of this evidence does, in fact, favor open classrooms. (1987, 22)

In a comprehensive review of effective open education, Giaconia and Hedges (1982) "support the view that open education programs *can* produce greater self-concept, creativity, and positive attitude toward school" (p. 600). Of particular interest is the finding that diagnostic evaluation appeared in all the programs that showed substantial effects on self-concept and creativity. These programs were not always the ones with the highest achievement test scores. Because of the diagnostic evaluation techniques (where evaluation was used to guide learning, teachers' record keeping was a combination of jotting in class and thoughtful writing about each child, charting rather than grading individual progress toward specific goals), "these students were not accustomed to competitive testing situations. For this reason, the students may have performed poorly on the standardized achievement tests that were used as dependent variables" (pp. 600–601) in these studies. Kamii's (1990) recent publication *Achievement Testing in the Early Grades: The Games Grown-Ups Play* reinforces informal evaluation techniques as most beneficial to children's construction of knowledge. We believe that such techniques are also most effective in facilitating the development of creative potential for precisely the same reasons: they emphasize learning over performance, intrinsic motivation, and child-initiated learning.

Interpreting the findings of meta-analyses, studies that attempt to combine the data and results of many smaller studies into one comprehensive analysis of open classroom environments, is difficult because the variables that define the classrooms, the teachers, and the children differ across the studies. Individual studies must be looked at cautiously as well, because the findings may not always be generalizable to other situations. For the most part, though, this research supports the efficacy of the open classroom concept as a means of developing creative potential. But how the concept is implemented remains a concern for early childhood educators.

Curricula are most effective when teachers promote and initiate concepts. *Teachers* must be intrinsically motivated to change. Unlike teachers in the open classroom movement, *today's teachers understand the reasons behind the change.* They value curious, experimenting children and are therefore more likely to interpret curricula and develop teaching methods that facilitate creativity. Most importantly, though, teachers are beginning to be empowered to implement their ideas throughout the curriculum. In short, the implementation of developmentally appropriate practices in today's preschool and primary classrooms may be successful *because teachers understand the theory, the principles of child development upon which it is based. As a result, they have the commitment necessary to implement it effectively.*

CURRICULA TO ENCOURAGE CREATIVE THINKING

Visual Imagery

Visual imagery is described as "the power to see things through the 'mind's eyes' . . . [to] create a mental picture of almost anything whenever we wish" (Osborn 1963, 30). Osborn describes three kinds of visual imagery: speculative—children create pictures in their minds of things never really experienced; reproductive imagination—children bring pictures back into the mind; and structural visualization—children are encouraged to bring a flat picture into the form of a three-dimensional object. Visual imagery activities may come easily to imaginative children who enjoy fantasy. An uninhibited, freewheeling style is an asset in stretching imagination, yet all children may participate in their own way in creative visualization activities (Fugitt 1986).

To go one step farther, we can construct activities with the power to *feel* things through the mind's eye. In Barbara Juster Esbensen's *The Man, the Cat, and the Sky* (Esbensen 1989 [found in a popular first grade reading series]), a wise, old Chinese man and his cat Cream would "listen to the blue wind blow over the grass." This phrase, like many that occur incidentally in every classroom everyday, provides an opportunity to seize the *creative moment.* "Close your eyes and think about the *blue* wind. What does it make you think of? How does it make you feel?" Children spontaneously use words like "soft," "easy," and 'lazy." "Now, what if you imagine a *gray* wind, etc.?" The rest of this beautiful Chinese story is about the visual image of changing clouds. To expand on this idea, record children's responses (without judgment of their quality), then follow up with children's drawings, poems, and stories about the wind or clouds. These followup activities will be rich in visual imagery and even metaphor, by virtue of the few incidental minutes taken to *stretch the story.*

Creative Dramatics

Ideas for creative dramatics in the classroom are readily available in early childhood professional publications. Drama is imaginative play in which free movement and sense impressions help children grow in creative awareness and self-confidence (Grossblatt 1980). Most teachers are familiar with creative dramatics, but a few guidelines[6] may be helpful:

- Remember that drama is for its participant, while theater is for the audience (i.e., the focus is on process not production) (Grossblatt 1980).
- Warm-up activities might include charades or games in which children make facial imitation of emotions (Necco, Wilson, and Scheidemantel 1982).
- Puppets may serve as actors and actresses in creative dramatics without exposing children to physical and verbal communication before an audience (Necco et al. 1982). Likewise, shadow play with puppets provides a novel approach for creative expression (McNeil 1981; Wisniewski 1986).
- When children have learned to act out the sequence of favorites such as "The Three Bears" or "Jack Be Nimble," encourage them to improvise on the story and act out new ideas (e.g., "How many ways can you think of for Jack to get over the candlestick?" (Schickedanz, York, Stewart, and White 1990).
- Creative dramatics should remain flexible so that children may easily accommodate to unexpected

---

[6]Additional references include Hunt and Renfro (1982), McCaslin (1975), and Sutton-Smith and Sutton-Smith (1974).

changes. What better way for children to "personal-
ize" an activity.

• Creative dramatics may be integrated into the
curriculum by extending activities through creative
dialogue techniques (Yawkey 1986).

Pantomime is another form of creative dramatics that is
underused as a classroom tool. Without words, how many ways
can you say "Thank you" or "I feel great!" or "Our
neighborhood has many helpful people"? Pantomime may be
built into many activities across the curriculum (Freericks 1980).

Music, Movement, and Art

Music, movement, and art are often called the "creative
arts." Although an effort has been made throughout this
monograph to demonstrate that creativity is an integral part of
the curriculum throughout the day, the areas of music,
movement, and art should also be highlighted. When planning
activities, teachers should apply the principles presented in this
chapter.

Music may be planned as an exploration of sounds to
acquire knowledge and skills leading to playful experimentation
with instruments and rhythms, melodies, and lyrics. Movement
may also provide opportunities for children to explore and define
the movement of their bodies in relation to the space around
them. One physical education teacher provides many opportunities for playful exploration of balls before she begins formal
instruction in control and handling of the ball. When skills are
developed, children form small groups and create routines using
their skills, often incorporating scarves, wands, or hula hoops in
their ball-handling routines.

Art activities that encourage children to explore various
media and processes are most likely to encourage creative
potential. Experimenting with the properties of watercolors and

brushes, watching the colors run together and blend, is far more valuable than making a watercolor "picture." Even second and third graders can become very frustrated in their attempts to make this media cooperate with their developing desire to approximate reality in their artwork. Second graders created a very striking bulletin board using their watercolor washes as the soft mosaic background against a foreground of black abstract designs that they cut out while listening to classical music. Consider the following media and focus on process when planning art activities: pastels, clay, scratch board, resists, tempera, collage, found-object collage, assemblage, sculpture, printing inkblots, charcoal and erasers, and watercolor markers.

Computers as Creativity Machines

Computer-aided instruction is an established component of modern education. Children of the 21st century *will* use computers as an integral part of their daily life. Like other teaching methods, the impact of computer-aided instruction on children's creativity is increasingly relevant. Papert (1980) reminds educators to be cautious of *using the computer to program the child.* Appropriately, *the child should program the computer* and "in doing so, acquire . . . a sense of mastery over a piece of the most modern and powerful technology and establish . . . an intimate contact with some of the deepest ideas from science, from mathematics, and from the art of intellectual model building" (Papert 1980, 5). Children who are plugged into computers to do drill and practice engage in convergent thinking. In fact, these programs are just another version of convergent board work or ditto sheets. Children who engage the computer with LOGO programs or learn to operate a mouse are open to the world of programming and computer graphics (*creating* with the sophistication of advanced technology) (Tan 1985). Writing stories, "painting" pictures, or engaging in problem solving are all facilitated by good software. Computers allow for playfulness and systematic exploration. The one-on-one of the child-to-computer permits risk-taking and opportunities to try different tasks without external evaluation. In choosing early childhood computer software, teachers should critically evaluate the ways in which and the extent to which the software provides opportunities for divergent thinking.

Retitling Old Stories
or Naming Original Works

Another incidental teaching technique involves creating imaginative names for stories or artwork or social studies projects. Any story provides a starting place for asking children to think of a different title and then to create their own book jacket. In fact, anything can be titled or retitled, once children realize the accepting atmosphere for this kind of thought.

One teacher had children think of names for the trees in the school yard. The children were encouraged to examine each tree, touch it, think about it, and then to think of a number of original names for it. Again, there was no evaluation of ideas during the process of generating the possible names. Children were encouraged to think of many names and then, later, to judge the name they liked the best. The real beauty of this activity is that many school yards have enough trees for everyone to "name one."[7]

Group Brainstorming

Brainstorming, though not a new idea (Osborn 1963), is often underused in classrooms. This is because, in the rush of the

---

[7]After naming their tree, several children in this class chose to write a story about it. This incidental teaching activity turned into a child-initiated unit on trees with children gathering information, writing about and illustrating their knowledge of trees. In the best of scenarios this idea became an integrated unit, including elements of reading, spelling, writing, and art; and engaging the cognitive, affective, and physical domains of development.

moment, it appears easier for the teacher to solve the problem for the children than to take the time to let the children solve it for themselves. Yet situations occur throughout the day when it takes only a minute to capitalize on the creative moment with techniques such as group brainstorming.

"How many ways can we think of to get from our room to the cafeteria without making any noise?" This is a real problem, defined in real terms, and the ideas for solving it yielded real solutions for a class of first graders. The children were at circle time when they began to generate a list of ways to stay quiet on the way to lunch.

According to Osborn, the ground rules for brainstorming are as follows:

Criticism is ruled out. Adverse judgment of ideas must be withheld until later.

Freewheeling is welcomed. The wilder the idea, the better; it is easier to tame down than to think up.

Quantity is wanted. The greater the number of ideas, the more likelihood of useful ideas.

Combination and improvement are sought. Participants should suggest how ideas of others can be turned into *better* ideas; or how two or more ideas can be joined into still another idea. (1963, 156)

How do we get from our room to the cafeteria? First, ideas were recorded on a flip chart: crawl like a snake (make hissing noises only); take the long way around, through the school yard to the front entrance of the school and then to the cafeteria; pretend we are elephants wearing soft slippers (this idea was the result of combining two ideas); put tape on everyone's mouth before we leave; eat lunch in our room. The ideas were displayed in the room and each day one of the workable ones was tried and its success was evaluated. The nonconformist's ideas were respected and tried along with other more conventional ideas. In addition, children's sense of humor became evident as everyone enjoyed "funny" ideas. The list grew throughout the year. There were many ways to get to lunch without disturbing the rest of the school.

Creative Problem Solving

It is impossible to discuss curriculum ideas for the classroom without mentioning Creative Problem Solving (CPS). Several methods of programmed instruction for CPS are well known—for example, *The Productive Thinking Program* (Covington, Crutchfield, and Davies 1972), *The Purdue Creative Thinking Program* (Feldhusen, Treffinger, and Bahlke 1970), and *Creative Problem Solving* (Parnes, Noller, and Biondi 1977; Noller, Parnes, and Biondi 1976). These programs clearly outline the five steps of CPS: fact finding, problem finding, idea finding, solution finding, and acceptance finding.[8] Any adult who has actually experienced the creative problem-solving process, usually in a workshop or retreat format, will attest to how easily these steps may be applied in an early childhood classroom. Yet, like so many other teaching methods, we may have to try it, to *experience it*, before we will attempt it in our classroom.

Several authors have translated the CPS model for early childhood educators, so we will not detail them here. The Play and Problem-Solving Model (see Figure 5, p. 58) provides guidelines for incidental teaching of problem-solving skills to preschool and early elementary age children (Tegano et al. 1989). Curriculum materials dealing with CPS for the primary grades are also available (Duling 1983; Eberle 1977; Ricca and Treffinger 1982).

---

[8]For more information, see Steps to Creative Problem Solving in the Appendix.

Productive Thinking

Many curriculum guides (e.g., teacher's guides for reading series) include a section called productive thinking with questions for children, asking them to use the content of the lesson in a divergent or creative way. These ideas may serve as a springboard for teachers to develop the ability to create their own productive thinking exercises.

Common among productive thinking exercises is the "Uses" question: "In what *new* ways could we use this as it is?" "How could this be modified to fit a new use?" (Osborn 1963, 232) or 'How could this be improved?" These simple questions and others such as "In what ways might I . . . ?" may appear to be teaching gimmicks, but they have a sound theoretical basis.

Freaky Fridays

One elementary school decided to set aside one day each month to celebrate creativity. Throughout each day of the year creativity was encouraged, but it was valued highly enough to let children know that teachers and administrators dedicated at least one day a month to creative thinking.

A corollary to this kind of special day is "backwards day" or "opposites day" when everything is done in reverse. What better way to show children the power of breaking a mindset about having to do things in a certain way. *Habit is one of the worst enemies of creativity.* Teachers who set the standard for valuing creativity by taking a chance on a "crazy" idea may influence the expression of creative potential by many children.

Novel Toys and Materials

High-interest materials spark exploration and play. Novel materials seem to bring out children's curious and questioning dispositions naturally. As children enter elementary school, it becomes more difficult to find truly novel materials.

Safe industry by-products or leftovers may be an excellent source of such materials, as well as working examples of recycling. One company donated a box of 3" X 3" flat plastic squares that were the genesis of many activities: "How might we use these squares?" Another teacher had access to discarded mat board from a local frameshop. These materials were used in a variety of activities throughout the year, from making raised relief maps to constructing buildings for a mock community to art projects. A computer manufacturer donated thousands of loose computer keys to a first grade classroom. These small, plastic squares with letters, numbers, and symbols were the center of many creative activities throughout the year. Finding materials, then, is only half the task; recognizing the potential in a variety of unstructured materials takes a keen eye. Early childhood educators have always been accused of being scavengers—a compliment when interpreted in light of the relationship of novel materials to creativity.

SUMMARY

Creativity is a process, an integral part of the curriculum. Creativity is fun. Looking for ways to incorporate creative learning into all parts of the day makes learning fun for children, as well as for teachers. Teachers and administrators may approach curriculum guides as outlines of knowledge and skills to be learned, rather than as strict instructions for how to teach.

Organizing a classroom to promote creative thinking involves planning by the teacher, the interactions of the children, and the involvement of the teacher. By understanding how the structure level of an activity is related to the potential for creative thinking, teacheres can use common-sense guidelines for modifying curricula to encourage creative thinking.

Understanding the role of exploration and play in the process of creative thinking and problem solving is the most critical step for teachers in understanding how experiential learning and creative thinking go hand-in-hand. It is important that teachers become critical observers of children's thinking processes as they work through the curriculum. In this way, they can become adept at facilitating the process of divergent thinking and deferring judgment to the process of creative problem solving (see Figure 5, the Play and Problem-Solving Model). With these skills teachers will be empowered to trust their understanding of the teaching/learning process, to articulate *why*, as well as *how*, to develop and interpret curricula in the context of their own classrooms.

Finally, the research on model programs and creativity tells us that *there are teaching methods that foster the development of creative potential in the early childhood classroom.* There is, however, no recipe or formula for making these methods work effectively in the classroom. The "creative curriculum" is really an attitude that begins with the teacher's ability to interpret curriculum and recognize and capitalize on the creative moment. Torrance devoted much of his life to educational research on creativity. As he puts it:

> Each teacher's way of teaching must ultimately be his [or her] own unique invention. I wish for you the very greatest success in perfecting your own invention—your way of teaching. (Torrance 1967, 187)

Chapter 4

THE TEACHER: ATTITUDES AND STYLES THAT FOSTER CREATIVE POTENTIAL

A classroom full of *thinking* students might be in sharp contrast to many classrooms today. What would you do if you saw a student in class leaning on his hand like Rodin's classic statue, *The Thinker,* with that strange look on his face? You might say, "Johnny, what are you doing?" If Johnny were honest, he might answer, "thinking." Some teachers might then be tempted to say, "Well, stop thinking, and listen to me!" What would you do? (Taylor 1963, 5)

When we ask teachers to behave in certain ways we must take their values into consideration. We have devoted a tremendous amount of thought and energy to trying to understand the learner; it is time we begin, with as much care, to examine the teacher. (Myers and Torrance 1961, 159)

Regardless of the nature of the child, and the materials or curriculum available to the child, the teacher is a powerful and influential factor in encouraging creative thinking. In Lucy's Project described in Chapter 3, Lucy realized that her role as an observer and facilitator of creative potential was a critical, ongoing process. In the Developmental-Ecological Model of Creative Potential in Young Children (Sawyers et al. 1990), discussed in Chapter 1, the contextual variables that include the *teacher,* mediate the biological and cultural influences and the influence of the individual child's cognitive and personality traits.

Hennessey and Amabile tell us: "It is clear from case studies that an environment conducive to creative production is not easily established, and once achieved, it must be constantly reshaped and controlled" (1987, 12). In other words, creating the psychologically safe environment described by Carl Rogers (1954) is not a formula; it is an *attitude*. As a teacher in a recent seminar remarked, "Oh, now I see, teaching for creativity is not a curriculum model, it's a whole philosophy of education."

The teacher creates the psychologically safe environment where learning is valued over performance, where the value of internal motivation is recognized, where teachers are astute observers of the process of exploration, play, and problem solving, and where teachers recognize the potential of their personal teaching style for facilitating or inhibiting the development of creative potential.

LEARNING OBJECTIVES VERSUS PERFORMANCE OBJECTIVES

Consider the following goals for a second grade class:

"Today, I want to see how good you are at doing these money problems."

or

"Today I want to see how much you can learn about using money."

Which goal is more likely to provide opportunities for creative thinking in a second grade classroom? For young children, creative thinking is viewed in terms of the *process of learning* rather than the *products of performance*. Likewise, these two statements illustrate the difference between teachers' perceptions of curriculum goals in terms of *learning* and *performance* (Dweck 1986; Katz and Chard 1989). An environment in which teachers interact with children based on their goals for *learning* is more suitable for encouraging creative potential.

88

A mathematics lesson on money is just one example of the wonderful opportunities for children to explore the many roads to the right answer (Kamii and Kamii 1990; Kamii and Rosenblum 1990). Children are encouraged to think of and share many ways of arriving at the answer, and to change and redefine the money problems to present new and original challenges to themselves and their classmates. Even with a subject like mathematics, which many may consider rote, teachers can find opportunities to encourage problem finding and creative problem solving. Teachers observe children's alternative routes toward mastery of a mathematics concept in the process of learning (where learning and performance are complementary processes), rather than having children memorize a set of steps to arrive at the right answer (performance only).

With performance goals (". . . how many you can get right"), teachers are forced to rely on formal assessments of children's knowledge and skills (unit tests, achievement tests) in which the child must demonstrate proficiency by producing the right answers (". . . how *good* you are at doing money problems"). Teachers who understand learning goals rely on formal and *informal* assessment techniques (observation and notes) to determine *how much* the child has learned and *in what ways* the child is learning about money. This involves participation. In a mathematics lesson, for example, the process of discovery learning, of finding and solving problems, is an observable process, an informal assessment of *how* the child is learning. When one focuses on learning, performance become a natural by-product.

Clorinda and her second grade classmates are working on math with the teacher in a small group. The goal is to provide opportunities for the children to construct a beginning understanding of multiplication. One of the examples deals with the familiar activity of washing clothes. The teacher explains that everyday the child wears a shirt and a pair of pants to school—two pieces of clothing. Everyday the family washes two pieces of clothing. The children in the groups are drawing their shirt and pants for the day. Now, how many shirts and pants will there be if there are two children in the family? They draw two children with two sets of clothes. The children pose the next question: "How many pieces of clothing if there are three children in the family?" They try to construct the answers to this question through drawing. Suddenly, Clorinda jumps up excitedly. "Gosh, there are six kids in my family. Now I understand why my mom says all she does is wash clothes!"

Clorinda's answer (performance) may not have been accurate when she began to calculate two pieces of clothing for six children, but what is important is that she began to understand (learn) about multiplication.

THE TEACHER'S ROLE AS OBSERVER

Structuring early childhood environments includes planning activities and centers designed to optimize children's learning by providing opportunities for children to cycle through exploration and play and to engage in creative problem solving. Structuring learning environments, then, is based on teachers' *observations* of children's play (Manning and Sharp 1977). Observation skills go hand-in-hand with daily planning and teacher involvement in activities. In a report of a three-year preschool project on play at the University of Sussex, Manning and Sharp underscore the interplay of teaching and observing:

Successful teacher involvement is entirely dependent on observation; e.g., only by observing will a teacher know how to help children solve a problem, be able to work out whether they will understand the solution, and know whether their interest is sufficient to warrant further experiment. In other words, she [or he] will have different objectives for different children at different times. She [or he] will not expect children to pursue problems that require thinking of a kind that they are not able to cope with. Nor will she [or he] want them to continue activities long after they have explored all the possibilities. (1977, 18)

Teachers often have no formal training in observation or in how to use observational data in their daily planning. Yet most teachers learn early in their careers that good observation skills are critical to individualizing learning episodes to meet the diverse needs of the children in their classroom. Informal observation skills become an integral part of successful teaching. We would advocate that teacher training programs give more attention to these skills in the classroom.

Let's go back to Lucy's use of observation to evaluate her modified lessons where she directed her attention to the quantity (fluency) and quality (originality) of the children's ideas. This provided her with a key insight into the process of creative thinking. Although not mentioned, it is likely that Lucy also observed individual differences in the children's approach to the tasks, noting how she might provide for future experiences at different structure levels for different children.

Good observation skills naturally lead to a heightened awareness of the individual personality and cognitive traits of children. The Preschool Creativity Rating Scale (see Appendix) may be an effective means for raising teachers' awareness of how creativity may be seen in the classroom. It may serve as a vehicle for reframing children's behaviors in the context of creative potential. Take, for example, a teacher who is having trouble understanding five-year-old Rachel's nonconformity. Sometimes Rachel's own ideas alienate her from the other children, as when she decided to paint snow*men* instead of a snow*man*. Although within the parameters of permissible activity at the art table, Rachel did not choose to paint one large snowman as all her classmates did; rather she chose to turn the paper in the other direction and paint eight or nine small snowmen falling to the ground as snowflakes. Rachel was willing to take the risk to try the picture her way, though several children in the class "reported" her behavior to the teacher. Observing Rachel's behavior against the backdrop of creativity enables her teacher to respect her originality and to pay closer attention to how Rachel thinks in other situations. It also provides the perfect opportunity to develop a sense of respect for individuality among Rachel's peers as well.

As observers, we bring with us all the biases of our training and experience with children. Objectivity is difficult to achieve when a teacher is, by definition, an integral part of the dynamics of a classroom. But objectivity may not be the appropriate goal in our observation of children. Identifying the perspective of the observer may be more useful to the educative process. Knowing from what perspective we are observing in a classroom, we gain insight into how our individual personalities and teaching style influence what we see. For example, three different teachers may have observed Rachel painting and had three different reactions. Ms. Steiner may have been impressed with the fine motor control necessary to paint the smaller snowmen. Mr. Morrow may have been concerned that the sideways picture wouldn't fit on the bulletin board with the other children's pictures. And Ms. Childers may have noticed that Rachel appeared unconcerned about the other children who were telling the teacher that her picture was the "wrong way." All three observations are valid perceptions of the same situation. If they are not truly objective observers, then, perhaps teachers may recognize how they view their classrooms—*from what personal perspective do they make their observations?* In this way they may heighten their awareness of the positive indicators of creativity.

By learning about ways to facilitate the creative potential of young children, educators are constantly reminded of the critical role of the teacher as an observer. How teachers observe creativity, though, hinges on the individual characteristic of the teacher in any given situation.

TEACHER CHARACTERISTICS THAT FACILITATE CREATIVE DEVELOPMENT

All teachers bring a set of personal teaching characteristics to the classroom. These characteristics may play a part in the way teachers motivate children, use rewards and encouragement, and view children's success in school. In addition, these characteristics may influence how teachers observe children, how they view the importance of time and schedules, and how and when they interact with children. By becoming aware of how their personal characteristics influence day-to-day interactions with children, teachers can begin to find ways to encourage *every* child's creative potential. This section outlines the teacher characteristics of playfulness, ambiguity tolerance, and interactive style.

Playfulness and Creativity

Teachers have firsthand understanding of the role of play in the lives of the children in their care. We have already reviewed both theoretical and empirical literature documenting the relationship of play and creativity. But are teachers of young children likely to acknowledge playfulness in their own lives?

Bettye Caldwell (1985) tells us that adult play is likely to be more convergent, structured, and governed by rules than children's play. Adults may say that they are going to "play" tennis, yet when they do so, there is no resemblance to what we observe when young children play. Caldwell discusses the "play paradox": adults may be less likely to play *with* children; instead they assume the role of *teaching* children how to play. She says:

> We're talking about having adults, who don't know how to play, teach children, who know quite well how to play. In other words, if we want to improve the play of children, we're using the wrong teacher. We're using people whose play is not at all playful (1985, 169).

Teachers who are playful may be more likely to play *with* children. Likewise, playful teachers are more likely to observe children's play from the children's perspective; they may also find situations in which they can be role models for exploration, divergent thinking, problem finding, and problem solving—that is, creativity.

How Playful Are You?

Playful teachers have a natural advantage for facilitating creativity in the children in their class. The following list is adapted from the description of playfulness as a psychological construct by Rubin, Fein, and Vandenberg (1983):

1. Playful teachers are guided by *internal motivation.*
2. Playful teachers are oriented toward *process.*
3. Playful teachers attribute their *own meanings* to objects or behaviors and are not bound by what they see.
4. Playful teachers focus on *pretend* ("what if" or "as if").
5. Playful teachers seek *freedom from externally imposed rules.*
6. Playful teachers are *actively involved.*

There is a natural match between playfulness and creativity. Teachers who are aware of these traits may be more likely to enter children's play with no expectation for the outcome, thus providing a relaxed, evaluation-free play environment. Contrast this to the less playful teacher who plans a play activity with a very narrow performance goal in mind and then directs the children's play toward that goal. We can recall an example of a teacher who wanted to teach numbers to her three-year-olds by playing dominoes:

The teacher arranged all 16 children in a circle, each with four dominoes. After placing the first domino in the center, she explained the rules of the game—match your number to the number on the end of the domino sequence; if your number

94

didn't match, you must wait until your next turn. The first three children stood up and then sat down—none of their dominoes provided a match. The fourth child matched the numbers. As the sequence continued, more often the next child missed a turn instead of matching the numbers. Finally, one boy stood up and placed the number three on his domino next to a three in the middle of the domino sequence. The teacher quickly pointed out that this was not allowed since he could match the domino only at the end of the sequence. Soon after that, the activity time was over and the outdoor time began.

The less playful teacher, although well intentioned because of a concern for performance objectives, is less likely to become part of the children's play, to defer judgment of children's ideas, or to encourage creative thinking, problem solving, and learning. Clearly, what was needed in this case was flexibility. The teacher could have adapted her activity to encourage greater participation and involvement by the children.

Playfulness, like other personality traits, comes in many degrees and forms. Teachers and administrators may recognize how playfulness affects their teaching or administrative styles. One principal's response to a third grade teacher sums up this personality trait. The discussion was about the best way to work with a novel approach to teaching a particular subject. The principal was encouraging the teacher to try the new approach. But the teacher was not sure whether to steer away from the traditional method, and perhaps was somewhat fearful of negative evaluation (mostly self-evaluation). In a playful attempt to allay the teacher's second thoughts, at least about the possibility of external evaluation, the principal responded, "Hey, I see in colors!" One might guess that most playful teachers also "see in colors."

How Much Do You Appreciate Humor?

Humor and creativity are related as "cognitive playfulness" (Ziv 1988). Humor was briefly mentioned in Chapter 2 as a possible trait of children with creative potential. Teachers may also look to themselves as a source of humor in the classroom. When a child "cracks a joke," capitalizing on the incongruity in a situation, the classroom relaxes as everyone enjoys the funny moment. This relaxed atmosphere is analagous to the "playful set" (Dansky and Silverman 1975) that is most conducive to creative thinking. Ziv tells us there is "convincing evidence that increased exposure to humor can increase one's level of creativity. . . . Teachers who would like to develop divergent thinking in their students should try and bring humor into the school" (1988, 114).

How Well Do You Tolerate Ambiguity

The ability to cope with unstructured or open-ended situations seems a natural requisite for creativity. Teachers are often presented with open-ended classroom situations where there is no apparent right answer or where confusion dominates for a period of time. Many early childhood activities are open-ended by nature. Some teachers may be very comfortable with these activities; others may be less comfortable. For example,

A cardboard box sculpture is an activity that may take several days to complete, with the planning of trial-and-error models, gluing, painting, and decorating. The classroom or a part of the classroom may be in disarray throughout the week. Ms. Rios, who is comfortable with ambiguous situations, will observe the process throughout the week and find satisfaction in anticipating the variety of children's sculptures. But Ms. Young, who is less comfortable with ambiguous situations, is likely to make suggestions about how the children might finish their sculptures, bringing closure to the activity and organization back to this part of the classroom. This teacher might also be less likely to think in terms of probability ("How might these children use these materials to make creative sculptures?"), focusing more on closure—the end product.

Extreme inability to tolerate ambiguity in an early childhood classroom is likely to be detrimental to the creative expression of children, yet most teachers recognize that they fall somewhere between the two ends of the continuum from very tolerant to very *in*tolerant of ambiguous situations.[9] Tolerance for ambiguity is one of the personal characteristics that teachers may look for in themselves. When they recognize ambiguity tolerance, they naturally begin to understand how this characteristic influences classroom interactions and the climate for creative expression.

Ambiguity Tolerance

Ambiguity tolerance may be important to the relationship of playfulness and creativity discussed earlier (Tegano 1990). In a study of 50 early childhood teachers, ambiguity tolerance and playfulness were highly correlated ($r = .80$). In fact, both ambiguity tolerance and playfulness were significantly correlated to creativity. Furthermore, more teachers with high scores on both ambiguity tolerance and playfulness also were found to have perceiving and intuitive personalities (Tegano and Catron 1990). On the Myers-Briggs Type Indicator (Myers and McCaulley 1985), a personality indicator, *perceiving teachers* are described as *spontaneous, flexible, and likely to adapt to events. Intuitive teachers* are described as *perceiving possibilities, relationships, and meanings of experiences.* It appears that teachers who enjoy ambiguous situations are more likely to be *flexible* in the classroom, to allow time for children's ideas to simmer, and to be *less directive* and *less evaluative* in their interactions with children—all characteristics likely to enhance the climate for creative expression.

---

[9]Persons who are tolerant of ambiguity have a "tendency to perceive ambiguous situations as desirable" (Budner 1962, 28). Individuals who are intolerant of ambiguity are described as "disinclined to think in terms of probability" (Frenkel-Brunswik 1948, 268) and have been found to solve problems without adequate information (Millon 1957).

The following questions will help teachers determine their own levels of ambiguity tolerance:

1. Do you plan, facilitate, and enjoy open-ended situations in the classroom? At what level of openness are you most comfortable?

2. How long can you tolerate confusion or open-endedness? What kind of ambiguous situations are comfortable or uncomfortable?

3. How do you react in ambiguous situations? What happens when you reach your individual level of tolerance (i.e., what is the nature of your interactions with children)? How does this affect the classroom climate for creative expression?

Chaotic Classrooms

Finding order from chaos is identified as a characteristic of creative persons (Tardiff and Sternberg 1988). But too much chaos *is* chaos, and it may fall short in providing the safe and predictable environment needed by young children. Ambiguity, on the other hand, is not only unavoidable but is also appropriate in an early childhood classroom.

An example from Edison's youth clearly illustrates the need for rules and organization—that is, a psychologically safe environment where both student and teacher (in this case, mother) are comfortable. Bryan reports:

In the cellar of the house he [young Edison] assembled materials for his first laboratory. Among these were 200 bottles, carefully arranged on shelves and all labeled POISON. "My mother's ideas and mine differed at times," he once said, "especially when I got experimenting and mussed up things." Indeed, Mrs. Edison ordered the removal of the laboratory—two hundred bottles and all; but she finally compromised the matter by allowing the "mess" to continue, provided it was kept under lock when "Al" was absent. (10, 9–10)

Thus, a delicate balance exists between providing a psychologically safe environment in which children and teachers feel comfortable planning for and dealing with ambiguous situations, and one that allows order to emerge without undue risk. For an environment that fosters creative potential, ambiguity tolerance is a teacher characteristic that augments both creative process and creative productivity.

Interactive Style:
Reacting vs. Responding

Consider the following classroom scenario:

Several children are transferring items from the mathematics center to the art table. They have taken the set of cutout felt numbers to the art table, which is covered with the materials of the ongoing art project (paper, scissors, glue, and glitter). The teacher may choose either to react or respond:

Possible REACTION: "Those felt numbers will get ruined on the art table. Please take them back to the math center."

Possible RESPONSE: "How are you planning to use the felt numbers? What might happen to them if you put them near the glue and glitter?"

Most of us would agree that the *response* is more appropriate than the *reaction*. However, in the heat of the moment, most teachers react rather than respond. The difference here is *time*. To respond with the more appropriate reply means that the teacher has built in some "hang time" before responding to a classroom situation.

How do we learn to build in hang time and what type of teacher is most likely to respond to classroom situations instead of reacting to them? Teachers who have developed good observation skills are more likely to understand how hang time benefits creative development. The process of observation provides the time to ascertain motives, predict what might happen next, approach the situation without evaluation—deferring judgment—and encourage children to define and solve a developing problem.

As discussed in the sections on playfulness and ambiguity tolerance, how teachers interact with children is closely related to personality. Some people are, by nature, more impulsive, while others are reflective. Reflective teachers are more able to sit back and observe children and defer judgment until they have gathered all the pertinent information about a situation. Impulsive teachers are more likely to be in the midst of the situation, with a more "do it" or "try it" approach.

Judging or Perceiving

Another way to look at interactive style is Jung's (1923) personality type of judging or perceiving.[10] Jung hypothesized that people differ in temperament and demonstrate a preference for the way they perceive and the way they make judgments (Myers 1980). Judging persons prefer the order and control over events that come with decisiveness and closure; perceiving persons prefer the flexibility and adaptability that come with keeping options open. The teacher who *reacts* to situations may be less likely to tolerate ambiguity and is therefore more likely to be a judging type. The perceiving-type teacher, on the other hand, may be more likely to *respond* playfully in ways that permit flexibility and adaptability, like the teacher who asked the children what they were going to do with the numbers in the art center. This perceiving-type teacher may also be more likely to let

---

[10]Jung's theory of personality includes four types: extroversion-introversion, sensing-intuitive, thinking-feeling, judgement-perception. The Myers-Briggs Type Indicator was developed from Jung's theory to assess these personality types. Information on how to use the Myers-Briggs Type Indicator with teachers may be found in *Teacher Types and Tiger Stripes* by G. D. Lawrence.

the children determine the nature of the problem and think through the possible solutions or compromises. This teacher may be more likely to give the children control over the situation.

All these responses (asking questions, adapting to the situation, letting children think through the problem) are conducive to children's creative thinking and learning. The reactions (telling children what the problem is and how to solve it, one right solution leading to closure, teacher control over the situation) are not likely to encourage children to think creatively or solve problems.

Possibilities or Practicalities

The intuitive personality type who sees possibilities, relationships, and meaning of experiences is more likely to encourage creative thinking in young children than is the sensing type who focuses on the immediate, real, practical facts of experience. In the example of the felt numbers on the art table, the sensing-type teacher might see the immediate danger of ruining the felt letters with glue, glitter, scissors, etc. The intuitive-type teacher might search for the possibilities that the children have seen in combining the materials of two "unrelated" centers. One teacher would react to the immediate situation while the other would be considering how to facilitate the generation of children's ideas toward a workable compromise— keeping the felt numbers on an adjacent shelf away from the mess or providing a clean space nearby where the numbers might be used without danger of being ruined.

Understanding Individual Style

Perceiving and intuitive characteristics are related to creativity in adults. Teachers with high scores on perception and intuition also had high scores on the trait of playfulness (Tegano and Catron 1990). Teachers who scored high on creativity also scored high on playfulness, with ambiguity tolerance playing an integral part in this relationship (Tegano 1990). By combining the traits of intuitive and perceiving individuals with our understanding of playfulness and ambiguity tolerance, we are able to compile a set of traits that characterize teachers who facilitate creative potential:

- They are likely to read between the lines for the possibilities that come to mind.
- They have the capacity to see future possibilities, often creative ones.
- They are open to new evidence and new developments, more curious than decisive.
- They show an interest in the new and untried, as well as a preference for learning new materials through an intuitive grasp of meaning and complexities.
- They are more focused on working with theory and imagination than dealing with tangibles and practical details.
- They adjust easily to the accidental and the unexpected.
- They exhibit flexibility, adaptability, and tolerance. (Lawrence 1987; Myers 1980; Tegano and Catron 1990)

In a classic study with the Minnesota Bureau of Educational Research, Torrance examined the responses of 114 teachers of children in public and private schools in 14 states. Myers and Torrance concluded:

Even though the teacher possesses knowledge of the kinds of situations which can provide him [or her] with opportunities to show respect for creative thinking, he [or she] must be alert to the occurrence of these situations, which means he [or she] must be receptive to theories about encouraging young people to be imaginative or to trust in themselves, and these traits are closely associated with the values which many teachers have. (1961, 158)

On the opposite end of the continuum, Torrance enumerated 10 characteristics found in teachers who could *not* apply one or more principles presented to them for accepting and supporting creativity. They were authoritarian, defensive, dominated by time, insensitive to their students' intellectual and emotional needs, lacking in energy, preoccupied with their information-giving functions, intellectually inert, disinterested in promoting initiative and self-reliance in their pupils, preoccupied with disciplinary matters, and unwilling to give much of themselves in the teaching-learning compact (Myers and Torrance 1961).

Keep in mind that no one teacher embodies all the traits on either end of the continuum; there are many variations on how these traits might be seen in any group of teachers. Also keep in mind that impulsive, sensing, judging teachers do not necessarily have adverse affects on creative development of children. A few judging-type and sensing-type teachers were also found to score high on playfulness and ambiguity tolerance (Tegano and Catron 1990). What is important here is understanding how one's personality (e.g., low tolerance for ambiguity, or lack of playfulness) affects the practices that influence children's creativity. All teachers, regardless of personality, can develop these practices, though they will be easier for some than for others. Teachers may:

- build in hang time before making decisions in order to respond and not react;
- consciously allow ambiguous situations to occur and keenly observe differences among children in the process of decision making;
- enter children's play as a participant with no expectations for the outcome of the episode;
- verbalize their own process of creative problem solving when everyday ambiguous situations naturally occur; and

103

- express genuine interest by following up on children's spontaneous ideas.

Passing some of the control to children can be a difficult process, but it reaps tremendous benefits.

The Elaborative Interactive Style

How, then, do these personality traits affect the way teachers interact with children to encourage creative thinking? Many decisions are made in classrooms everyday. In all likelihood, teachers do not have the luxury of consulting colleagues or leafing through a child development textbook when the story dramatization activity is falling apart. Many decisions must be made on the spot because a situation requires an immediate response. Thus, the teacher's style of interacting in the classroom may be as much a function of personality as of philosophy of education or training.

An interesting study by Wittmer and Honig (1989) demonstrated how important it is for teachers to be aware of this issue. Analyzing the types of questions teachers asked three-year-olds in child care centers, these researchers found that 32 percent of the questions were convergent with only one right answer (e.g., "What is this?") and 56 percent were simple yes/no questions (e.g., "Is this a table?"). Only 12 percent were divergent questions or questions that permitted choice (e.g., "Do you want milk or juice?" or "What do you want to do?"). In this environment, how can divergent thinking emerge?

In another study, kindergarten teachers were trained in asking questions to promote divergent thinking (Cliatt, Shaw, and Sherwood 1980). Questions were asked of children at learning centers, during outside play, and at snack time. Examples included: "What other things could you do with these materials?" "If you were lost in a forest what are some of the things you would do?" These teachers also planned activities to promote divergent thinking, such as open-ended stories or elaboration of pictures (e.g., "Why might the boy in the picture be smiling?"). In addition, these teachers received training in classroom management and self-concept buildup. Over an eight-week period, this group of teachers had 250 instances of divergent thinking, compared to less than 25 instances in a control group with no training. More importantly, the divergent thinking abilities of the children in the class with the trained teachers increased during that time. The researchers concluded:

> Not only can elementary-school-aged children improve their scores when trained in divergent thinking, but also very young children can realize dramatic increases when repeatedly exposed to divergent-thinking situations. If divergent thinking is truly a tool for solving problems, then it should be encouraged at an early age so that it becomes a natural and accepted part of children's intellectual functioning. (Cliatt, Shaw, and Sherwood 1980, 1063)

Teachers' style of interaction has been tied to playfulness and creativity in another context as well (Graham, Sawyers, and DeBord 1989). Teachers with various levels of experience were asked to consider a short classroom vignette and then to choose how they might respond, using structured, unstructured, or elaborative styles of interaction. For example:

> You have put out some red and blue playdough for the children. Jonathan squeezes some red and blue dough together.
>
> You might:
>
> Say, "Jonathan, we need to keep the red playdough separate from the blue so we can keep it nice." (Structured)
>
> Allow Jonathan to experiment making no comment on the mixing of the playdough. (Unstructured)
>
> Say, "Jonathan, look at the new color of playdough that you got when you mixed the red with the blue." (Elaborative)

105

Teachers in this study were given five seconds to consider each response separately and then decide if they might respond in this way. They also rated themselves on a playfulness scale and were administered a creativity test.

The student teachers in this study who were more playful were also more creative and showed a preference for an elaborative interaction style. More experienced teachers' preference for the structured interaction style was related to low creativity. Note that the strongest relationship of playfulness with creativity and elaborative style was found for student teachers. The student teachers reported one to two years of experience, while the classroom teachers averaged three to six years of experience. It is unclear what happens to teachers as they gain experience in the classroom, but this study indicates that experiences with children may alter the relationship between interactive style, creativity, and playfulness. More information is needed to provide insight into how teachers' interactive style is related to their playfulness and personality traits discussed earlier, as well as how teachers may influence the development of creative thinking in the classroom.

In yet another study, preschool and kindergarten teachers were observed as they interacted with children at two free-choice centers (Tegano, May, Lookabaugh, and Burdette 1991). These teachers' interactions were recorded and classified along two dimensions: evaluative/facilitative and directive/nondirective. Figure 6 shows how these two dimensions make four interactive styles. Interestingly, all teachers' interactions were easily coded into one of the four quadrants. Nondirective/facilitative teacher comments are thought to be helpful in facilitating children's creative processes.

Figure 6
Teacher's Verbal Interaction

Four Quadrants

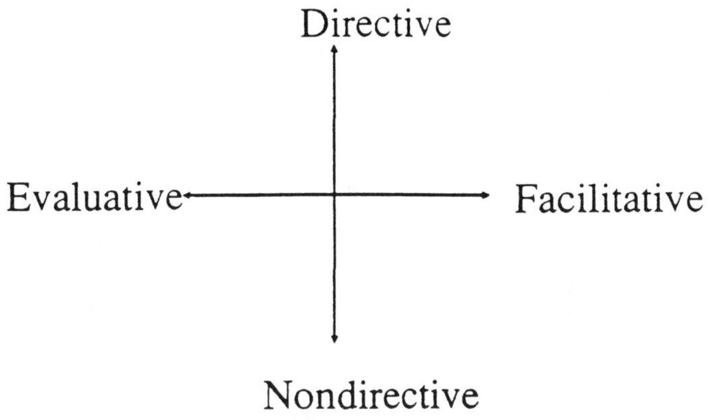

Directive

Evaluative ———————— Facilitative

Nondirective

Directive -   teacher control, directing
                     child's activity

Nondirective -   child control, open-ended
                     questions, echo child's
                     thought or idea

Evaluative -   teacher's opinion, positive or
                     negative

Facilitative -   informative, giving
                     information, elaborative

Four-year-olds Shane and Harrison were spurred on in a problem-solving episode by Shane's *facilitative/nondirective comment:*

> Harrison was making a rainbow with markers and left the table saying that he was going to get a black marker to make a black stripe in his rainbow. Shane remarked that there is no black in a rainbow. Harrison responded, "Yes, there is!" Rather than let this deteriorate into a "Yes-there-is, No-there-isn't" confrontation, Shane remarked, "Gee, I've never seen black in the rainbow."

The teacher seized the moment, asking the boys if they'd like to help her find the prism. Eventually they also examined the resource books on rainbows.

One of the most difficult tasks of teaching is to ask more open-ended questions and to use nondirective comments that serve to facilitate rather than direct children's thinking. The paradox here may lie in the term "teacher" (Moran, Goble, and Bomba 1990). Our desire to fulfill our own expectations for the teacher role may lead us to be overly didactic and predominantly concerned with outcomes. To teach is to impart knowledge; to facilitate is to nurture children's construction of their own ideas. Both processes, teaching and facilitating, are means to the same end—children's achievement of the curriculum goals. Which of these processes is also likely to encourage children to explore their own ideas, to play with their ideas, to test their ideas, and to trust their ideas? Which of these processes is likely to prepare children to live with the complexities of the world they will inherit? What is difficult is to reconfigure the conception of teachers to allow for greater flexibility in the way they fulfill that role.

SUMMARY

The teacher is the central figure in determining how and to what extent an optimal environment for creativity may occur in an early childhood classroom. If we accept that biological, cultural, personality, and cognitive traits are influenced by the environment, then the teacher, who is by and large responsible for the environment, plays a critical role in the development of creative potential.

Creativity is fostered in classrooms where learning is valued over performance, where teachers are trained to observe and understand children's play and interactions in the classroom, where ambiguous situations are tolerated by teachers at least for a period of time, where teachers engage children in playful interchange, and, in fact, where teachers value their own creativity. In this psychologically safe classroom questions are respected, judgment is deferred, and the source of motivation comes from within the child. The teacher sets the tone for this environment; consequently, the individual personality traits and teaching style of the teacher become salient in the endeavor to foster the creative potential of the children in the classroom.

Chapter 5

PUTTING IT ALL TOGETHER

> All men have the stars . . . but they are not the same thing for
> different people. For some, who are travelers, the stars are
> guides. For others they are no more than little lights in the sky.
> For others, who are scholars, they are problems. (Saint
> Exupéry1943, 85)

"Putting it all together" to optimize creative potential in young children is not an easy task. There are no shortcuts, no clear-cut ready-made gimmicks for encouraging creative thinking in young children. There are no easy formulas for teaching creative reading or mathematics or social studies to children. As with most areas of development (cognitive or social), creative development will happen in an integrated fashion. Just as we cannot successfully separate children's learning into language arts, mathematics, science, and expressive arts, or into cognitive, affective, and physical domains, neither can we successfully separate creative development into curricular areas or developmental compartments.

As we watch the pendulum of education research swing back and forth, we sometimes believe that the new findings are really old ideas with new names. As cyclic and confusing as the world of educational research may seem to be, teaching to the whole child remains the most consistent finding. We may attach a different label—teaching to the whole child or integrated learning—but the central idea remains clear.

Like other aspects of the child, creativity follows a developmental sequence. With young children we are focused on the process of generating ideas. With increased skills and knowledge, primary grade children begin to be concerned about the product of their creative endeavors. Older children engage in self-evaluation of their creative products, while adult creativity is characterized by societal judgment.

Ten years of research has left us with a relatively short "list" of ideas for how best to create the psychologically safe environment that is critical for optimal creative development. Detailed explanations, documentation, and examples of how *the child, the curriculum,* and *the teacher* impact the psychologically safe environment are thoroughly discussed in this monograph. To put it all together, then, is to briefly summarize and succinctly emphasize the most salient ideas in the monograph.

THE CHILD

Creativity is a developmental process. For young children, certain characteristics are discernible, though certainly no one child is likely to display all of them. The cognitive characteristics of the creative young child include fantasy, divergent thinking, metaphoric thinking, attention to detail, task persistence, and curiosity.

There is clear empirical validation that creativity and intelligence are separate constructs during the early childhood years. Thus teachers should be cautious in assuming that precocious children are necessarily creatively gifted, especially at the expense of failing to encourage the creative child who may not stand out as a young scholar.

The personality traits associated with creativity in the early years are an easy temperament, nonconformity, risk-taking, and motivation that comes from within the child and is not driven by external rewards. Nearly all children display some of these characteristics at some time or other. We interpret this as an indication that *all* young children have creative potential.

THE CURRICULUM

Creativity and curriculum complement each other. The curriculum is a *guide* to the knowledge and skills that are necessary to develop creative thinking skills. The curriculum provides the content around which creativity may develop. *How* the content is presented to the child is the means to creative development. Dramatic play areas, writing centers, or science tables all provide settings to encourage this development.

Exploration and play in these activity areas are the basis for creative problem solving and lifelong learning. Creative thinking is fostered in classrooms where children are given opportunities to explore new materials and ideas, play with these materials or ideas, and construct new knowledge and skills. The process of exploration and play is not confined to preschool and kindergarten classrooms; it also exists in the journals kept by third graders or students in college literature and biology classes.

The following questions for presenting curriculum to young children may serve as a guide:

- Is the concept developmentally appropriate?
- Are the children intrinsically interested in it?
- Are materials provided for the children to explore and think about?
- Are there opportunities for divergent thinking?
- Are there opportunities for children to interact and communicate with peers and adults?

Implicit in these guidelines is the role of the teacher in planning activities, the role of the individual child in structuring activities to meet his/her needs, and the concomitant role of the teacher in facilitating creative thinking throughout the day.

Some ideas for presenting curricula to children in ways that foster creative thinking include visual imagery, creative dramatics and pantomime, productive thinking, computer thinking games, interesting and novel materials or ideas, and emphasizing divergent thinking. These teaching techniques require that teachers understand the process of learning and articulate *why,* as well as *how,* to interpret curricula.

112

THE TEACHER

The teacher is a powerful and influential factor in encouraging creative development. Creativity is fostered in an environment where children have a clear understanding of the limits (i.e., order not chaos); where they feel secure in exploration and play behaviors within those limits; where learning is valued over performance; and where children's internal motivation is understood as the basis of learning.

Personal teaching style is influenced by individual personality traits. Teachers should look closely at how their personal teaching style may affect creativity and thus become *aware* of subtle changes in their attitude or behavior that might make a big difference in the psychologically safe atmosphere of the classroom. Playfulness, ambiguity tolerance, and interactive style have been discussed as recognizable traits conducive to creative development that influence the classroom atmosphere.

15 KEY POINTS

Figure 7 gives 15 key points for optimizing creative potential in young children.

After attending a workshop on creativity during which most of these 15 points had been discussed, one teacher astutely observed that "I do most of these things already in my classroom. What I've learned here today is how these things work together to help children develop creatively." Indeed! Early childhood teachers with play-based or experientially based programs are masters in the art of observing, listening to children's ideas, deferring judgment, individualizing, and promoting the development of healthy self-concepts.

The concepts outlined in this monograph are all relevant in preparing children to live in tomorrow's world. The 21st century promises vague, ill-structured, and complex problems. Knowledge and skills centered on convergent solutions will not suffice. Perhaps the most telling criticism of our schools

Figure 7
Key Points for Optimizing
Creative Potential in Young Children

1. Find ways for creativity to traverse the whole curriculum and the whole child.
2. Incorporate and adapt to children's interest and ideas.
3. Provide a variety of materials for exploration and play.
4. Facilitate pretend play, fantasy, and other ways and means to imagination.
5. Help children focus on their own special talents or strengths.
6. Encourage children to take part in the decision-making process. Allow them to have control of their learning experiences, and thus develop confidence in their control of their own learning.
7. Be part of a warm, supportive atmosphere and a climate of mutual respect and acceptance—a psychologically safe classroom with the freedom and security necessary for individual or group exploration and creative thinking.
8. Allow children time to think about and develop their ideas. Very few problems are solved immediately or spontaneously.
9. Accept unusual ideas and responses of children. Show children that their ideas have value. Encourage them to be proud of their own ideas.
10. Treat children's questions with respect.
11. Avoid unnecessary rewards/reinforcement.
12. Suspend judgment and evaluation of children's attempts at creative thinking.
13. Encourage children to guide and evaluate their own work. Avoid competition.
14. Facilitate the creative process by stopping to observe; then respond (not react) in elaborative ways, asking open-ended questions, providing resources, participating without predetermined expectations in children's activities.
15. SHOW CHILDREN THAT YOU VALUE CREATIVITY (children's creativity as well as your own)!

Adapted from Block 1984; Feldhusen and Treffinger 1980; Hennessey and Amabile 1987; Tegano et al. 1989; and Torrance 1962.

throughout the educational reform movement that erupted in the latter part of the 1980s is that students are not able to think critically and thus will not be adequate to the task of adapting to the world as it exists today and as it will exist tomorrow. Yet, it appears to us, these are the very skills that have been part of quality early childhood programs over the past decade. Attention to the creative potential of young children lays the foundation for future critical thinking. Children will face situations where the divergent thinking skills learned now will strengthen the critical thinking skills to be developed later and empower today's children to solve tomorrow's problems.

For many readers, the insights gained from this monograph will be simply the *reframing of good teaching habits by an increased knowledge of how children develop creative thinking skills*. As such, the information presented here is not intended to revolutionize early childhood education, but rather to apply knowledge of developmentally appropriate practice for children to an understanding of the development of creativity in the early years. A teacher who read an early draft of this monograph developed an important realization: "After reading this I felt as if I could say, 'I can do this in my classroom without hours of preparation.' " Indeed, much of what is discussed here is already happening in many classrooms and perhaps, more importantly, most of the ideas can be easily incorporated into classrooms without a large investment in time or money. It is the reframing of these ideas under the umbrella of creativity that makes them work.

After completing a two-week workshop on creativity and early education, one of our teachers provided this insight that has stayed with us:

It's as though I've gone through a door marked *CREATIVITY*. As I walk through the corridor, I pass many smaller hallways filled with what is known about how to encourage creativity in my classroom. I walk right by some of the hallways because it's old stuff. At others, I stop and spend some time to learn. At the end of the hallway, I'm given a new pair a glasses to wear. These new glasses help me integrate everything I've seen. Now, when I go back to my classroom, I can take off my old glasses and put on my new ones. I can see children's learning and development from a new perspective.

Helping children learn in creative ways, facilitating children's creative thinking skills, makes teaching a joyful activity. Or as the principal mentioned in Chapter 4 said, "I see in colors!" In facilitating the creative potential of all children, remember YOU *CAN* SEE IN COLORS!

APPENDIX

How to Kill Creativity

1. *Have Children Work for an Expected Reward*
   The expectation of reward can actually undermine intrinsic motivation and creativity of performance. . . . A wide variety of rewards has now been tested, and everything from good-player awards to marshmallows produces the expected decrements in intrinsic motivation and creativity of performance. . . . For students who initially display a high level of interest in a task, an expected reward . . . makes them much less likely to take risks or to approach a task with a playful or experimental attitude.

2. *Set Up Competitive Situations*
   If you want to be absolutely certain that your students' motivation and creativity will be undermined, set up a situation in which they must compete among themselves for some desirable reward or other form of recognition.

3. *Have Children Focus on Expected Evaluation*
   When faced with an upcoming evaluation of their performance, students are likely to adopt an extrinsic motivational orientation. Their focus is turned away from the intrinsically enjoyable aspects of the task itself, and the creativity of their performance is undermined. . . . Prior evaluation [has] an overall negative impact on creativity of performance—even though the evaluation was positive.

4. *Use Plenty of Surveillance*
   The mere presence of a watchful audience can be all it takes to undermine intrinsic interest and creativity of performance. . . . Watch [students'] every move, and shift their focus away from the task at hand and toward your implied evaluation of their progress.

5. *Set Up Restricted-Choice Situations*
   Nursery school children were asked to make a paper collage. Children assigned to the choice condition were allowed to choose any 5 out of 10 boxes of materials to use in this task. An experimenter made the selections for the children in the no-choice condition. All subjects then completed their collages, which were rated on creativity by artists. As predicted, there was a substantial difference in collage creativity. The collages made by subjects in the choice condition were judged significantly more creative than were those made by subjects in the no-choice condition.

From *Creativity and Learning,* by Beth A. Hennessey and Teresa M. Amabile (Washington, D.C.: National Education Association, 1987), 11–15.

Preschool Creativity Rating Scale

Directions: Please indicate the degree to which each description or adjective typifies the child. How typical of the child is each behavior?

(1) Never; (2) Rarely; (3) Sometimes; (4) Frequently; (5) Always

Comments

1. Child is willing to take risks, do things differently, try new things. Willing to try the difficult.   (1)   (2)   (3)   (4)   (5)

2. Child has an extraordinary sense of humor in everyday situations.   (1)   (2)   (3)   (4)   (5)

3. Child is opinionated, outspoken, willing to talk openly and freely.   (1)   (2)   (3)   (4)   (5)

4. Child is flexible, able to accommodate to unexpected changes in situations.   (1)   (2)   (3)   (4)   (5)

5. Child is self-directed, self-motivated.   (1)   (2)   (3)   (4)   (5)

6. Child is interested in many things, is curious, questioning.   (1)   (2)   (3)   (4)   (5)

7. Child engages in deliberate, systematic exploration, develops a plan of action.   (1)   (2)   (3)   (4)   (5)

8. Child is able to make activities uniquely his or her own, personalizes what he or she does.   (1)   (2)   (3)   (4)   (5)

9. Child is imaginative, enjoys fantasy.   (1)   (2)   (3)   (4)   (5)

10. Child is a nonconformist, does things his or her own way.   (1)   (2)   (3)   (4)   (5)

11. Child comes up with many solutions to a problem.   (1)   (2)   (3)   (4)   (5)

12. Child is uninhibited, has a freewheeling style.   (1)   (2)   (3)   (4)   (5)

For more information on use of this scale, please contact Dr. Deborah Tegano, Department of Child and Family Studies, University of Tennessee, Knoxville, TN 37996-1900.

Steps to Creative Problem Solving

1. *Fact Finding*
   Take the "Mess," the feeling of uneasiness, puzzlement, knowing something is wrong, and begin making sense of it. Gather *facts* that will help in making sense of the "Mess."

2. *Problem Finding*
   Begin to sort out the facts. Many problems may become apparent. Look at the "Mess" from many different perspectives. Identify the problem (or a variety of subproblems).

3. *Idea Finding*
   Select a problem statement and generate many ideas, alternatives, or solutions. Defer judgment and never rule out any idea, no matter how farfetched or silly.

4. *Solution Finding*
   Determine the criteria or standard for judging ideas. Generate many criteria and choose the one(s) most appropriate for judging the ideas. The most promising ideas or solutions can be determined.

5. *Acceptance Finding*
   Develop a Plan of Action. What are the steps that need to be taken to implement the solution? What are the possible obstacles along the way? Create alternatives or strategies for a plan for creative action. This is a very important part of the process of Creative Problem Solving.

Adapted from "Creative Problem Solving for Gifted and Talented Students," by D. J. Treffinger and S. J. Parnes, *Roeper Review* 2, no. 4 (1980): 31.

BIBLIOGRAPHY

Amabile, T. *The Social Psychology of Creativity*. New York: Springer-Verlag, 1983.

Barron, F. "Putting Creativity to Work." In *The Nature of Creativity*, edited by R. J. Sternberg. New York: Cambridge University Press, 1988.

Barron, F., and Harrington, D. H. "Creativity, Intelligence and Personality." *Annual Review of Psychology* 32 (1981): 439–76.

Block, J. H. "Making School Learning Activities More Playlike: Flow and Mastery Learning." *Elementary School Journal* 85 (1984): 65–75.

Bomba, A., and Moran, J. D., III. "The Relationship of Selected Temperament Characteristics to Creative Potential in Preschool Children." *Early Childhood Development and Care* 41 (1989): 225–30.

Bredekamp, S., ed. *Developmentally Appropriate Practice in Early Childhood Programs Serving Children from Birth Through Age 8.* Washington, D.C.: National Association for the Education of Young Children, 1987.

Broberg, G. C., and Moran, J. D., III. "Creative Potential and Conceptual Tempo in Preschool Children." *Creativity Research Journal* 1 (1988): 115–24.

Brophy, J., and Choquette, J. "Divergent Production in Montessori Children." Paper presented at the Biennial Meeting of the Society for Research in Child Development. Philadelphia, March 1973.

Bruner, J. "Vygotsky: A Historical and Conceptual Perspective." In *Culture, Communication, and Cognition: Vygotskian Perspectives*, edited by J. V. Wertsch. New York: Cambridge University Press, 1985.

Bryan, G. *Edison, the Man and His Works*. New York: Knopf, 1926.

Budner, S. "Intolerance of Ambiguity as a Personality Variable." *Journal of Personality* 30 (1962): 29–50.

Caldwell, B. "Parent-Child Play: A Playful Evaluation." In *Play Interactions: The Role of Toys and Parental Involvement in Children's Development*, edited by C. C. Brown and A. W. Gottfried. Skillman, N.J.: Johnson and Johnson, 1985.

Carnegie Forum on Education and the Economy. *A Nation Prepared: Teachers for the 21st Century.* Washington D.C.: Carnegie Foundation, 1986.

Chaille, C., and Barber, L. "The Dilemma for Teachers." In *Achievement Testing in the Early Grades: The Games Grown-Ups Play,* edited by C. Kamii. Washington, D.C.: National Association for the Education of Young Children, 1990.

Cliatt, M. J. Puckett; Shaw, J.; and Sherwood, J. "Effects of Training on the Divergent Thinking Abilities of Kindergarten Children." *Child Development* 51 (1980): 1061–64.

Cohen, S. "Exploratory Task Behavior and Creativity in Young Children." *Home Economics Research Journal* 2 (1974): 262–67.

Cohen, S., and Oden, S. "An Examination of Creativity and Locus of Control in Children." *Journal of Genetic Psychology* 124 (1974): 179–85.

Covington, M.; Crutchfield, R.; and Davis, L. *The Productive Thinking Program.* Columbus, Ohio: Merrill, 1972.

Cronin, L. "Creativity in the Science Classroom." *Science Teacher* 56, no. 2 (1989): 35–36.

Dansky, J. "Make-Believe: A Mediator of the Relationship Between Play and Associative Fluency." *Child Development* 51 (1980a): 576–79.

_____. "Cognitive Consequences of Sociodramatic Play and Exploration Training for Economically Disadvantaged Preschoolers." *Journal of Child Psychology and Psychiatry* 20 (1980b): 47–58.

Dansky, J., and Silverman, I. "Effects of Play on Associative Fluency in Preschool-aged Children." *Developmental Psychology* 11 (1973): 104.

DeVries, R. *Programs of Early Education: The Constructivist View.* New York: Longman, 1987.

DeVries, R., and Kohlberg, L. *Constructivist Early Education: Overview and Comparison with Other Programs.* Washington, D.C.: National Asociation for the Education of Young Children, 1990.

Dimidjian, V. J., ed. *Play's Place in Public Education for Young Children.* Washington, D.C.: National Education Association, 1991.

Dreyer, A., and Rigler, D. "Cognitive Performance in Montessori and Nursery School Children." *Journal of Educational Research* 62 (1969): 411–16.

Dudek, S. "Creativity in Young Children—Attitude or Ability?"

Journal of Creative Behavior 8 (1974): 282–92.

Duling, G. *Creative Problem-Solving for an Eency Weency Spider.* Buffalo: D.O.K. Publishers, 1983.

Dweck, C. "Motivational Processes Affecting Learning." *American Psychologist* 41 (1986): 1040–48.

Dweck, C., and Leggett, E. "A Social-Cognitive Approach to Motivation and Personality." *Psychological Review* 95 (1988): 256–73.

Eberle, R. *Scamper Games for Imagination Development.* Buffalo: D.O.K. Publishers, 1977.

Esbensen, B. J. "The Man, the Cat, and the Sky." In *A New Day.* Morristown, N.J.: Silver Burdette and Ginn, 1989.

Feldhusen, J. F., and Treffinger, D. J. *Creative Thinking and Problem-Solving in Gifted Education.* Dubuque: Kendall/Hunt, 1980.

Feldhusen, J. F.; Treffinger, D. J.; and Bahlke, S. "Developing Creative Thinking: The Purdue Creativity Program." *Journal of Creative Behavior* 4 (1970): 85–90.

Fosnot, C. T. *Enquiring Teachers, Enquiring Learners—A Constructivist Approach for Teaching.* New York: Teachers College Press, 1990.

Freericks, M. "Pantomime." *Instructor* 89, no. 7 (1980): 61–62, 67.

Frenkel-Brunswik, E. "Tolerance Toward Ambiguity as a Personality Variable." *American Psychologist* 3 (1948): 268.

Fugitt, E. "Creative Visualization Activities." *Day Care and Early Education* 13 (1986): 26–31.

Giaconia, R., and Hedges L. "Identifying Features of Effect on Open Education." *Review of Educational Research* 54, no. 4 (1982): 579–602.

Goodwin, M.; Sawyers, J. K.; and Barby, K. "The Effects of Exploration on Preschoolers' Problem-Solving Ability." *Journal of Genetic Psychology* 149 (1988): 317–33.

Gowan, J. C.; Demos, G. D.; and Torrance, E. P. *Creativity: Its Educational Implications.* New York: Wiley, 1967.

Graham, B.; Sawyers, J. K.; and Debord, K. "Teachers' Creativity, Playfulness, and Style of Interaction with Children." *Creativity Research Journal,* 1989.

Griffing, P.; Clark, P.; and Johnson, L. "The Relationship of Spontaneous Classroom Play and Teacher Ratings of Curiosity to Tested Curiosity in Preschool Children." Presentation at American Educational Research Association annual meeting,

New Orleans, April 1988.

Grossblatt, R. "Down with Plays." *Learning* 8, no. 7 (1980): 12–13.

Groves, M.; Sawyers, J. K.; and Moran, J. D., III. "Reward and Ideational Fluency in Preschool Children." *Early Childhood Research Quarterly* 2 (1987): 335–40.

Guilford, J. "The Structure of Intellect." *Psychological Bulletin* 53 (1956): 267–93.

Haddon, P., and Lytton, H. "Teaching Approach and the Development of Divergent Thinking Abilities in Primary School." *British Journal of Educational Psychology* 38 (1968): 171–80.

____. "Primary Education and Divergent Thinking Abilities: Four Years On." *British Journal of Educational Psychology* 41 (1971): 138–47.

Harrington, D. H. "The Ecology of Human Creativity." In *Theories of Creativity,* edited by M. A. Runco and R. S. Albert. Newbury Park, Calif.: Sage Publications, 1990.

Hawkins, D. "Nature Closely Observed." *Daedalus* 112, no. 2 (1983): 65–89.

Hedges, C.; Giaconia, R.; and Gage, N. "Meta-analysis of the Effects of Open and Traditional Instruction." Stanford, Calif.: Stanford University Program on Teaching Effectiveness, 1981.

Henderson, R. "Defining Goals in Open Education." In *Studies in Open Education,* edited by B. Spodek and H. J. Walberg. New York: Agathon Press, 1975.

Hennessey, B., and Amabile, T. *Creativity and Learning.* Washington, D.C.: National Education Association, 1987.

____. "The Conditions of Creativity." In *The Nature of Creativity,* edited by R. J. Sternberg. New York: Cambridge University Press, 1988.

Hunt, T., and Renfro, N. *Puppetry in Early Childhood Education.* Austin, Texas: Nancy Renfro Studios, 1982.

Hutt, C. "Exploration and Play." In *Play and Learning,* edited by B. Sutton-Smith. New York: Gardner Press, 1979.

Inagaki, K. "Relationships of Curiosity to Perceptual and Verbal Fluency in Young Children." *Perceptual and Motor Skills* 48 (1979): 789–90.

Jenkins, R., ed. *The Papers of Thomas A. Edison.* Baltimore: Johns Hopkins University Press, 1989.

John-Steiner, V. *Notebooks of the Mind.* Albuquerque: University of New Mexico, 1985.

Johnson, J.; Ershler, J.; and Bell, C. "Play Behavior in a Discovery Based and a Formal Education Preschool Program." *Child Development* 51 (1980): 271–74.

Jung, C. *Psychological Types.* London: Routledge and Kegan Paul, 1923.

Kamii, C. "Autonomy as the Aim of Education: Implications of Piaget's Theory." In *Number in Preschool and Kindergarten.* Washington, D.C.: National Association for the Education of Young Children, 1982.

_____. "Leading Primary Education Toward Excellence—Beyond Worksheets and Drill." *Young Children* 40, no. 6 (1985): 3–11.

Kamii, C., ed. *Achievement Testing in the Early Grades: The Games Grown-Ups Play.* Washington, D.C.: National Association for the Education of Young Children, 1990.

Kamii, C., and DeVries, R. *Physical Knowledge in Preschool Education: Implications of Piaget's Theory.* New York: Prentice-Hall, 1978.

Kamii, C., and Kamii, M. "Negative Effects of Achievement Testing in Mathematics." In *Achievement Testing in the Early Grades: The Games Grown-Ups Play,* edited by C. Kamii. Washington, D.C.: National Association for the Education of Young Children, 1990.

Kamii, C., and Rosenblum, V. "An Approach to Assessment in Mathematics." In *Achievement Testing in the Early Grades: The Games Grown-Ups Play,* edited by C. Kamii. Washington, D.C.: National Association for the Education of Young Children, 1990.

Karmiloff-Smith, A. "Children's Problem Solving." In *Advances in Developmental Psychology,* vol. 2, edited by M. E. Lamb, A. L.Brown, and B. Rogoff. Hillsdale, N.J.: Erlbaum, 1984.

Katz, L., and Chard, S. *Engaging Children's Minds: The Project Approach.* New York: Ablex, 1989.

Kogan, N. "Stylistic Variation in Childhood and Adolescence: Creativity, Metaphor, and Cognitive Style." In *Handbook of Child Psychology. Vol. 3, Cognitive Development,* edited by J. H. Flavell and E. M. Markman; series ed., P. H. Mussen. New York: Wiley, 1983.

Kogan, N.; Connor, K.; Gross, A.; and Fava, D. "Understanding Visual Metaphor: Developmental and Individual Differences." *Monographs of the Society for Research in Child Development* 45, no. 1 (serial no. 183), 1980.

Lawrence, G. D. *People Types and Tiger Stripes.* 2d ed. Gainesville, Fla.: Center for Applications of Psychological Type, 1987.

Lepper, M. R.; Greene, D.; and Nisbett, R. E. "Undermining Children's Intrinsic Interest with Extrinsic Reward: A Test of the 'Overjustification' Hypothesis." *Journal of Personality and Social Psychology* 28 (1973): 129–37.

Lieberman, N. J. "Playfulness and Divergent Thinking: An Investigation of Their Relationship at the Kindergarten Level." *Journal of Genetic Psychology* 107 (1965): 219–24.

_____. *Playfulness: Its Relationship to Imagination and Creativity.* New York: Academic Press, 1977.

Malgady, R. "Children's Interpretation and Appreciation of Similes." *Child Development* 48 (1977): 1734–38.

_____. "Metric Distance Models of Creativity and Children's Perception of Figurative Language." *Journal of Educational Psychology* 73 (1981): 866–71.

Manning, K., and Sharp, A. *Structuring Play in the Early Years at School.* London: Drake Educational Associates, 1977.

Marcos, G., and Moran, J. D., III. "Cross-Cultural Comparisons of Ideational Fluency in Preschool Children." *School Psychology* (1989): 199–204.

McCaslin, N. "Act Now! Plays and Ways to Make Them." New York: S. G. Phillips, 1975.

McCuller, J.; Fabes, R.; and Moran, J. D., III. "Does Intrinsic Motivation Theory Explain the Adverse Effects of Rewards on Immediate Task Performance?" *Journal of Personality and Social Psychology* 52, no. 5 (1987): 1027–33.

McGhee, P. "Development of the Creative Aspects of Humor." In *Children's Humor,* edited by P. McGhee and A. Chapman. New York: Wiley, 1980.

McGraw, K. O. "The Detrimental Effects of Reward on Performance: A Literature Review and a Prediction Model." In *The Hidden Costs of Rewards: New Perspective on the Psychology of Human Motivation,* edited by M. R. Lepper and D. Greene. Hillsdale, N.J.: Erlbaum, 1978.

McLloyd, V. "The Effects of the Structure of Play Objects on the Pretend Play of Low-Income Children." *Child Development* 54 (1983): 626–35.

McNeil, J. "Shadows That Light Up in the Classroom." *Teacher* (January 1981): 42–44.

Mednick, S. "The Associative Basis of the Creative Process." *Psychological Review* 69 (1962): 220–32.

Mehrotra, J., and Sawyers, J. K. "Creative Problem Solving in Indian Preschoolers." *Creative Child and Adult Quarterly* (1989): 147–54.

Meizitis, S. *Cognitive Style, Exploratory Behavior, and Verbal Fluency in Montessori and Non-Montessori Trained Preschoolers.* Toronto: Ontario Institute for Studies in Education, 1971.

Milgram, R. M., and Arad, R. "Ideational Fluency as Predictor of Original Problem Solving." *Journal of Educational Psychology* 73 (1981): 568–72.

Milgram, R. M.; Milgram, N. A.; Rosenbloom, G.; and Rabkin, L. "Quantity and Quality of Creative Thinking in Children and Adolescents." *Child Development* 49 (1978): 385–88.

Milgram, R.; Moran, J. D., III; Sawyers, J. K.; and Fu, V. R. "Original Thinking in Israeli Preschool Children." *School Psychology International* 8 (1987): 54–58.

Milgram, R. M., and Rabkin, L. "A Developmental Test of Mednick's Associative Hierarchies of Original Thinking." *Developmental Psychology* 16 (1980): 157–58.

Miller, B., Jr., and Archambault, J. *The Bugs, the Goats, and the Little Pink Pigs.* Allen, Texas: Developmental Learning Materials, 1987.

Miller, H., and Sawyers, J. K. "A Comparison of Self and Teachers' Ratings of Creativity in Fifth Grade Children." *Creative Child and Adult Quarterly* 3–4 (1989): 179–85.

Miller, L., and Dyer, J. "Four Preschool Programs: Their Dimensions and Effects." *Monographs of the Society for Research in Child Development* 40, no. 5–6 (serial no. 162), 1975.

Millon, T. "Authoritarianism, Intolerance of Ambiguity and Rigidity Under Ego and Task-Involving Conditions." *Journal of Abnormal and Social Psychology* 55 (1957): 29–33.

Moore, L., and Sawyers, J. K. "The Stability of Original Thinking in Young Children." *Gifted Child Quarterly* 31 (1987): 126–29.

Moran, J. D., III; Goble, C.; and Bomba, A. K. "The 'Teacher' Paradigm." Paper presented at the annual meeting of the Southern Association on Children Under Six, Dallas, March 1990.

Moran, J. D., III; Milgram, R.; Sawyers, J. K.; and Fu, V. R. "Original Thinking in Preschool Children." *Child Development* 54 (1983): 921–26.

Moran, J. D., III; Sawyers, J. K.; Fu, V. R.; and Milgram, R.

"Predicting Imaginative Play in Preschool Children." *Gifted Child Quarterly* 28, (1984): 92–94.

Moran, J. D., III; Sawyers, J. K.; and Moore, A. "The Effects of Structure in Instructions and Materials on Preschoolers' Creativity." *Home Economics Research Journal* 17 (1988): 148–52.

Myers, I. *Gifts Differing.* Palo Alto, Calif.: Consulting Psychologists Press, 1980.

Myers, I., and McCaulley, M. *Manual: A Guide to the Development and Use of the Myers-Briggs Type Indicator.* Palo Alto, Calif.: Consulting Psychologists Press, 1985.

Myers, I., and Torrance, E. "Can Teachers Encourage Creative Thinking?" *Educational Leadership* 19 (1961): 156–59.

Necco, E.; Wilson, C.; and Scheidemantel, J. "Affective Learning Through Drama." *Teaching Exceptional Children* 15 (1982): 22–25.

Nelson, K. *Making Sense: The Acquisition of Shared Meaning.* New York: Academic Press, 1985.

Nicholson, M., and Moran, J. D., III. "Preschool Teachers' Judgments of Four Year-Olds' Creativity." *Perceptual and Motor Skills* 63 (1986): 1211–16.

Noller, R. B.; Parnes, S. J.; and Biondi, A. M. *Creative Action Book.* New York: Scribner's, 1976.

Olszewski, P., and Fuson, K. "Verbally Expressed Fantasy Play of Preschoolers as a Function of Toy Structure." *Developmental Psychology* 18 (1982): 57–61.

Orlich, D. "Science Inquiry and the Commonplace." *Science and Children* 6 (1989): 22–24.

Osborn, A. *Applied Imagination: Principles and Procedures of Creative Problem Solving.* 3d ed. New York: Scribner's, 1963.

Papert, S. *Mindstorms: Children, Computers, and Powerful Ideas.* New York: Basic Books, 1980.

Parnes, S.; Noller, R.; and Biondi, A. *Guide to Creative Action.* New York: Scribner's, 1977.

Pellegrini, A. "The Effects of Exploration and Play on Young Children's Associative Fluency: Review and Extension of Training Studies." In *Child's Play: Developmental and Applied,* edited by T. Yawkey and A. Pellegrini. Hillsdale, N.J.: Erlbaum, 1984.

_____. "A Sequenced Questioning Paradigm as a General Facilitator of Preschoolers' Associative Fluency." *Perceptual and Motor Skills* 52

(1981): 649–50.

Penjon, R. "Le Rire et la Liberté." *Revue Philosophique* 2 (1891): 113–25.

Pepler, D. J., and Ross, H. S. "The Effects of Play on Convergent and Divergent Problem Solving." *Child Development* 52 (1981): 1202–10.

Piaget, J. *Play, Dreams, and Imitation in Childhood.* New York: Norton, 1962.

_____. *To Understand Is to Invent: The Future of Education.* New York: Grossman, 1973.

Pulaski, M. "Play as a Function of Toy Structure and Fantasy Predisposition." *Child Development* 41 (1970): 531–37.

Ricca, J., and Treffinger, D. *Adventures in Creative Thinking.* Buffalo: D.O.K. Publishers, 1982.

Rogers, C. "Towards a Theory of Creativity." *ETC: A Review of General Semantics* 11 (1954): 249–60.

Rogers, C.; Meeks, A.; Impara, J.; and Fray, R. "Measuring Playfulness: Development of the Child Behaviors Inventory of Playfulness." Paper presented at Southwest Conference on Human Development, New Orleans, April 1988.

Rogers, C. S., and Sawyers, J. K. *Play in the Lives of Children.* Washington, D.C.: National Association for the Education of Young Children, 1988.

Rogoff, B. "Integrating Context and Cognitive Development." In *Advances in Developmental Psychology,* vol. 2, edited by M. E. Lamb, A. L. Brown, and B. Rogoff. Hillsdale, N.J.: Erlbaum, 1984.

Rubin, K.; Fein, G.; and Vandenberg, B. "Play." In *Handbook of Child Psychology: Volume 4. Socialization, Personality, and Social Development,* edited by E. M. Hetherington; series ed., P. H. Mussen. New York: Wiley, 1983.

Runco, M. "Teachers' Judgments of Creativity and Social Validation of Divergent Thinking Tests." *Perceptual and Motor Skills* 59 (1984): 711–17.

Runco, M. A. "Interrater Agreement on a Socially Valid Measure of Students' Creativity." *Psychological Reports* 61 (1987): 1009–10.

Runco, M. A., and Albert, R. S., eds. *Theories of Creativity.* Newbury Park, Calif.: Sage Publications, 1990.

Saint Exupéry, Antoine de. *The Little Prince.* New York: Harcourt Brace Jovanovich, 1943.

Sawyers, J. K., and Moran, J. D., III. "Locus of Control and Ideational Fluency in Preschool Children." *Perceptual and Motor Skills* 58 (1984): 857–58.

Sawyers, J. K.; Moran, J. D., III; Fu, V. R.; and Horm-Wingerd, D. "Correlates of Metaphoric Comprehension in Young Children." Manuscript submitted for publication, 1991.

Sawyers, J. K.; Moran, J. D., III; Fu, V.; and Milgram, R. "Familiar Versus Unfamiliar Stimulus Items in Measurement of Original Thinking in Young Children." *Perceptual and Motor Skills* 57 (1983): 51–55.

Sawyers, J. K.; Moran, J. D., III; and Tegano, D. "A Theoretical Model of Creative Potential in Young Children." In *Expanding Awareness of Creative Potentials Worldwide,* edited by C. W. Taylor. Salt Lake City: Brain Talent-Powers Press, 1990.

Schickedanz, J.; York, M.; Stewart, I.; and White, D. *Strategies for Teaching Young Children.* 3d ed. Englewood Cliffs, N.J.: Prentice-Hall, 1990.

Schweinhart, L.; Weikart, D.; and Larner, M. "Consequences of Three Preschool Curriculum Models Through Age 15." *Early Childhood Research Quarterly* 1 (1986): 15–45.

Shaw, C. *It Looked Like Spilt Milk.* New York: Harper and Row, 1947.

Singer, J. L., ed. *The Child's World of Make Believe.* New York: Academic Press, 1973.

Slavin, R. E. "A Theory of School and Classroom Organization." *Educational Psychologist* 22, no. 2 (1987a): 89–108.

_____. "Developmental and Motivational Perspectives on Cooperative Learning." *Child Development* 58, no. 5 (1987b): 1161–67.

_____. *Grouping for Instruction: Equity and Effectiveness.* Baltimore: Center for Research on Elementary and Middle Schools, 1987c.

Smilansky, S. *The Effects of Sociodramatic Play on Disadvantaged Children: Preschool.* New York: Wiley, 1968.

Starkweather, E. "Creativity Research Instruments Designed for Use with Preschool Children. *Journal of Creative Behavior* 5 (1971): 245–55.

Sternberg, R. J., ed. *The Nature of Creativity.* New York: Cambridge University Press, 1988.

Strauss, S., ed. *U-Shaped Behavioral Growth.* New York: Academic Press, 1981.

Sutton-Smith, B. "Novel Responses to Toys." *Merrill-Palmer Quarterly* 14 (1968): 151–58.

Sutton-Smith, B., and Sutton-Smith, S. *How to Play with Your Children (and When Not To)*. New York: Hawthorn/Dutton, 1974.

Tan, L. "Computers in Preschool Education." *Early Child Development and Care* 19 (1985): 319–36.

Tardiff, T., and Sternberg, R. J. "What Do We Know About Creativity?" In *The Nature of Creativity*, edited by R. J. Sternberg. New York: Cambridge University Press, 1988.

Taylor, C. "The Creative Process and Education." *Instructor* 73 (1963): 5, 12.

Taylor, C. W. "Various Approaches to and Definitions of Creativity." In *The Nature of Creativity*, edited by R. J. Sternberg. New York: Cambridge University Press, 1988.

Tegano, D. "Relationship of Tolerance of Ambiguity and Playfulness to Creativity." *Psychological Reports* 66 (1990): 1047–56.

Tegano, D.; Bennett, E.; and Pike, G. "Constructing a Measure of Preschool Children's Creativity Through Social Validation." Manuscript submitted for publication, 1990.

Tegano, D., and Catron, C. "Early Childhood Educators: Encouraging the Creative Potential of Young Children." Manuscript submitted for publication, 1990.

Tegano, D.; May, G.; Lookabaugh, S.; and Burdette, M. "Quality of Teacher Interactions in Relation to Creativity." Unpublished data, 1991.

Tegano, D., and Moran, J. D., III. "Developmental Study of the Effects of Dimensionality and Presentation Mode on Original Thinking of Children." *Perceptual and Motor Skills* 68 (1989): 1275–81.

Tegano, D., and Parsons, M. "The Effects of Structure and Play Period Duration on Preschoolers' Play." Poster presented at the Society for Research in Child Development Biennial Meeting, Kansas City, Mo., April 1989.

Tegano, D.; Sawyers, J. K.; and Moran, J. D., III. "Play and Problem Solving: A New Look at the Teacher's Role." *Childhood Education* 66 (1989): 92–97.

Tegano, D. W., and Burdette, M. P. "Length of Activity Period and Play Behaviors of Preschool Children." *Journal of Research in Childhood Education* 5, no. 2 (1991).

Thomas, A., and Chess, S. *Temperament and Development*. New York: Brunner/Mazel, 1977.

Torrance, E. "Creative Teaching Makes a Difference." In *Creativity: Its Educational Implications,* edited by J. C. Gowan, G. D. Demos, and E. P. Torrance. New York: Wiley, 1967.

_____. "Testing the Educational and Psychological Development of Students from Other Cultures." *Review of Educational Research* 38 (1968): 77–94.

Torrance, E. P. *Guiding Creative Talent.* Englewood Cliffs, N.J.: Prentice-Hall, 1962.

_____. "Cross-cultural Studies of Creative Development in Seven Selected Societies." In *Creativity: Its Educational Implications,* edited by J. C. Gowan, J. Khatena, and E. P. Torrance. 2d ed. Dubuque, Iowa: Kendall/Hunt, 1981.

Treffinger, D., and Huber, J. "Designing Instruction in Creative Problem Solving: Preliminary Objectives and Learning Hierarchies." *Journal of Creative Behavior* 9 (1975): 260–66.

Treffinger, D.; Isaksen, S.; and Firestien, R. *Handbook of Creative Learning.* Vol. 1. Williamsville, N.Y.: Center for Creative Learning, 1982.

Treffinger, D. J., and Parnes, S. J. "Creative Problem Solving for Gifted and Talented Students." *Roeper Review* 2, no. 4 (1980): 31–32.

Vandenberg, B. "The Role of Play in the Development of Insightful Tool Using Abilities." Paper presented at the American Psychological Association meeting, Toronto, August 1978.

_____. "Play, Problem-Solving and Creativity." In *New Directions for Child Development—Children's Play,* edited by K. H. Rubin. San Francisco: Jossey-Bass, 1980.

Vosniadou, S., and Ortony A. "The Emergence of the Literal-Metaphorical-Anomalous Distinction of Young Children." *Child Development* 54 (1983): 154–61.

Walberg, H. "Improving the Productivity of America's Schools." *Educational Leadership* 41 (1984): 19–30.

Wallach, M., and Kogan, N. *Modes of Thinking in Young Children: A Study of the Creativity-Intelligence Distinction.* New York: Holt, Rinehart, and Winston, 1965.

Wallach, M., and Wing, C., Jr. *The Talented Student: A Validation of the Creativity-Intelligence Distinction.* New York: Holt, Rinehart, and Winston, 1969.

Wallach, M. A. "Creativity." In *Carmichael's Manual of Child Psychology,* edited by P. H. Mussen. Vol. 1. 3d ed. New York:

Wiley, 1970.

Ward, W. C. "Creativity in Young Children." *Child Development* 39 (1968): 737–54.

____. "Creativity? in Young Children." *Journal of Creative Behavior* 8 (1974): 101–6.

Webb, C. "Social and Impersonal Conformity and Creativity of Preschool Children." Master's thesis in progress, University of Tennessee, Knoxville, 1991.

Wisniewski, D. "Shadow Play." Workshop presented by Wolftrap Performing Arts Center at National Association for the Education of Young Children Conference, Washington, D.C., November 1986.

Wittmer, D., and Honig, A. "Convergent or Divergent? Teachers' Questions to Three-Year-Old Children in Daycare." Development Meeting, Kansas City, Mo., 1989.

Yawkey, T. "Creative Dialogue Through Sociodramatic Play and Its Uses." *Journal of Creative Behavior* 20 (1986): 52–60.

Young, Robert D. *Risk-Taking in Learning, K–3.* Washington, D.C.: National Education Association, 1991.

Ziv, A. "Using Humor to Develop Creative Thinking." *Journal of Children in Contemporary Society* 20 (1989): 99–116.

F